Jason Santa Maria

ON WEB TYPOGRAPHY

MORE FROM THE A BOOK APART LIBRARY

HTML5 for Web Designers
Jeremy Keith

CSS3 for Web Designers
Dan Cederholm

The Elements of Content Strategy
Erin Kissane

Responsive Web Design
Ethan Marcotte

Designing for Emotion
Aarron Walter

Mobile First
Luke Wroblewski

Design Is a Job
Mike Monteiro

Content Strategy for Mobile
Karen McGrane

Just Enough Research
Erika Hall

Sass for Web Designers
Dan Cederholm

Responsible Responsive Design
Scott Jehl

You're My Favorite Client
Mike Monteiro

Publisher: Jeffrey Zeldman
Designer: Jason Santa Maria
Editor-in-Chief: Mandy Brown
Editor: Tina Lee
Technical Editor: Nick Sherman
Copyeditor: Nicole Fenton
Proofreader: Caren Litherland
Compositor: Rob Weychert
Ebook Production: India Amos

ISBN: 978-1-9375570-6-5

A Book Apart
New York, New York
http://abookapart.com

10 9 8 7 6 5 4 3 2 1

TABLE OF CONTENTS

FOREWORD

BEFORE USERS start reading a single word of text on a website, they are already judging the typography. More than any other design element, type sends instant messages about a site's content and purpose. Is this digital environment designed for reading, shopping, or gaming? Is it meant for experiencing over time or cruising by in a minute or two? Is its primary function to lead you through a process (subscribing to a service or answering a survey), or does it aim to submerge you in content (reading an article, watching a video, or choosing a stock photo)? Typography—its size, style, and system—helps tell people what all this content is actually for.

The quality and tone of a website's typography also sends instant messages about the people who made the site. Good type makes you look good. Bad type makes you look bad. Good type inspires confidence and trust; bad type triggers disdain and disgust. We've all landed on a website that we immediately know is a dumping ground for stolen content and crappy ads. Without even reading that come-on for pimple cream or the latest work-at-home scheme, we're already hitting the back button in search of a more savory place to invest our time.

Jason Santa Maria's approachable guide to web typography narrates the thought process behind working with type, from choosing fonts to crafting hierarchies to building grids. Rather than handing down a list of rules and prohibitions, Santa Maria walks side by side with readers through a creative journey. He invites us to think about our own reading experience right now—as we peruse this book—by providing clear and compelling examples for visual comparison. We the readers get to judge and evaluate different styles, combinations, and configurations of type, applied to real text that we can picture in the real world.

Designing for the web should always consider the needs of the user. This book considers the needs of you: the reader of these pages. Whether you are a developer or a designer, a student or a professional, a veteran of the web or a secret lover of print, you will find inspiration and guidance in this wise and kindly book, written by one of the web's most respected typographic minds.

—Ellen Lupton

INTRODUCTION

IN THE 1977 documentary film *Powers of Ten,* designers Charles and Ray Eames investigate what makes up the structure of our world and the universe, from the smallest particles to the most vast collections of matter (http://bkaprt.com/owt/1/). The film starts by focusing overhead on a couple having a picnic on a one-square-meter blanket (FIG 1). From there, we zoom out at one power of ten (see?) every ten seconds, all the way out to 10^{24}—100 million light years from Earth. Then we retrace our path to the picnicking couple and delve through the powers of ten on a microscopic scale, down to 10^{-16} where quarks operate. The film shows how big things are made up of smaller things, and how the relationships of those smaller things are integral to forming the bigger ones. Even when we can't perceive them all at the same time.

When I first saw the film, I had an immediate revelation. It put to words and pictures things I had never verbalized. The way everything is connected, whether implicitly or explicitly, is the same way I approach typographic design.

I often work by zooming in and out between the general and the specific, orchestrating the tone and message of a design. Type is design's smallest atomic unit—the framework for everything we try to communicate with our boxes, grids, CSS properties, and the other elements that go into making a website.

Whether you move from largest to smallest or smallest to largest, these elements are spun from one another. The width of a grid column influences the line length of a paragraph. A typeface's contrast influences how small you can set that typeface so it's still legible on your phone. The tools we use and the choices we make affect a design up and down the supply chain.

It's this reflexive relationship that holds a design together—the design equivalent of gravitational force. Okay, maybe not that far, but typography is the craft of setting type to give language a visual form. Typography is a design's *voice.*

This idea informs the way I like to work and helps me take a relaxed and practical approach to typography. I don't mean I

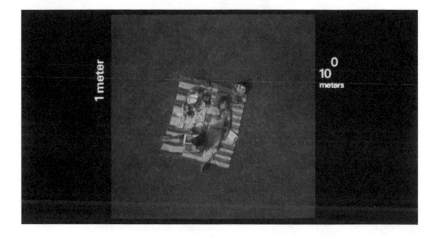

FIG 1: The documentary short, *Powers of Ten,* by Charles and Ray Eames, 1977.

haphazardly throw letters around on a page, but I do believe that developing a feel for typography trumps an encyclopedic knowledge of its history.

Are you with me? Good!

WHAT THIS BOOK WILL DO

Get ready, because I want to show you how to see type beyond a pretty set of letters with flourishes. To see in and around a typeface. To know how it speaks.

I want to show you how to get to know the myriad typefaces out there, evaluate them for different purposes, and understand how your choices affect the ways we read content and interpret design.

I want to show you ways to improve your typographic design *right now.* While typography is a centuries-old visual language, we need to see where it works and reinterpret where it falls short for the medium of the interactive screen, where to embrace old design methodologies, and where to diverge to create new ones.

I want to show you that even though this stuff can be difficult to wrap your head around, what you get back is well worth it. Being good at typography makes you a more adept thinker, communicator, and designer. When you immerse yourself in the fine details of text, you not only make yourself aware of those details and how they affect communication, but you also put yourself in your readers' shoes.

Typography is a craft that rewards ongoing practice. This book will help you understand how the language of typography adapts when applied to the web and how to choose good typefaces to support your designs.

And while this book is about typography for the web, it overlaps with a lot of good typographic methods that transcend any medium. We can distill good practices from the past, before type existed on glowing panels in front of our faces, and learn about specific considerations for the screen.

Don't just throw up your hands and use Helvetica (or, gasp!, Arial). You can do better than that, and I'll show you how.

What follows is my personal take on typography. It won't be the same as everyone else's, and some people may disagree with my approaches, but this represents most everything I've gleaned about designing with type. Some points may feel like common sense that don't merit a mention. Some concepts may seem minor on their own, but they add up. Typography is a practice of small improvements made in concert to create a whole better than the sum of its parts.

Take these things to heart, and you will get better with type.

HOW WE READ

I WANT YOU TO think about what you're doing right now. I mean *really* think about it. As your eyes move across these lines and funnel information to your brain, you're taking part in a conversation I started with you. The conveyance of that conversation is the type you're reading on this page, but you're also filtering it through your experiences and past conversations. You're putting these words into context. And whether you're reading this book on paper, on a device, or at your desk, your environment shapes your experience too. Someone else reading these words may go through the same motions, but their interpretation is inevitably different from yours.

This is the most interesting thing about typography: it's a chain reaction of time and place with you as the catalyst. The intention of a text depends on its presentation, but it needs you to give it meaning through reading.

Type and typography wouldn't exist without our need to express and record information. Sure, we have other ways to do those things, like speech or imagery, but type is efficient, flexible, portable, and translatable. This is what makes typography not only an art of communication, but one of nuance and craft, because like all communication, its value falls somewhere on a spectrum between success and failure.

The act of reading is beautifully complex, and yet, once we know how, it's a kind of muscle memory. We rarely think about it. But because reading is so intrinsic to every other thing about typography, it's the best place for us to begin. We've all made something we wanted someone else to read, but have you ever thought about that person's reading experience?

Just as you're my audience for this book, I want you to look at your audience too: your readers. One of design's functions is to entice and delight. We need to welcome readers and convince them to sit with us. But what circumstances affect reading?

READABILITY

Just because something is legible doesn't mean it's readable. *Legibility* means that text can be interpreted, but that's like saying tree bark is edible. We're aiming higher. *Readability* combines the emotional impact of a design (or lack thereof) with the amount of effort it presumably takes to read. You've heard of *TL;DR* (too long; didn't read)? Length isn't the only detractor to reading; poor typography is one too. To paraphrase Stephen Coles, the term readability doesn't ask simply, "Can you read it?" but "Do you want to read it?" (http://bkaprt.com/owt/2/).

Each decision you make could potentially hamper a reader's understanding, causing them to bail and update their Facebook status instead. Don't let your design deter your readers or stand in the way of what they want to do: *read.*

Once we bring readers in, what else can we do to keep their attention and help them understand our writing? Let's take a brief look at what the reading experience is like and how design influences it.

THE ACT OF READING

When I first started designing websites, I assumed everyone read my work the same way I did. I spent countless hours crafting the right layout and type arrangements. I saw the work as a collection of the typographic considerations I made: the lovingly set headlines, the ample whitespace, the typographic rhythm (**FIG 1.1**). I assumed everyone would see that too.

It's appealing to think that's the case, but reading is a much more nuanced experience. It's shaped by our surroundings (am I in a loud coffee shop or otherwise distracted?), our availability (am I busy with something else?), our needs (am I skimming for something specific?), and more. Reading is not only informed by what's going on with us at that moment, but also governed by how our eyes and brains work to process information. What you *see* and what you're *experiencing* as you read these words is quite different.

As our eyes move across the text, our minds gobble up the type's *texture*—the sum of the positive and negative spaces inside and around letters and words. We don't linger on those spaces and details; instead, our brains do the heavy lifting of parsing the text and assembling a mental picture of what we're reading. Our eyes see the type and our brains see Don Quixote chasing a windmill.

Or, at least, that's what we hope. This is the ideal scenario, but it depends on our design choices. Have you ever been completely absorbed in a book and lost in the passing pages? Me too. Good writing can do that, and good typography can grease the wheels. Without getting too scientific, let's look at the physical process of reading.

Saccades and fixations

Reading isn't linear. Instead, our eyes perform a series of back and forth movements called *saccades,* or lightning-fast hops across a line of text (**FIG 1.2**). Sometimes it's a big hop; sometimes it's a small hop. Saccades help our eyes register a lot of information in a short span, and they happen many times over the course of a second. A saccade's length depends on our proficiency as readers and our familiarity with the text's topic. If I'm a scientist and reading, uh, science stuff, I may read it more quickly than a non-scientist, because I'm familiar with all those science-y words. Full disclosure: I'm not really a scientist. I hope you couldn't tell.

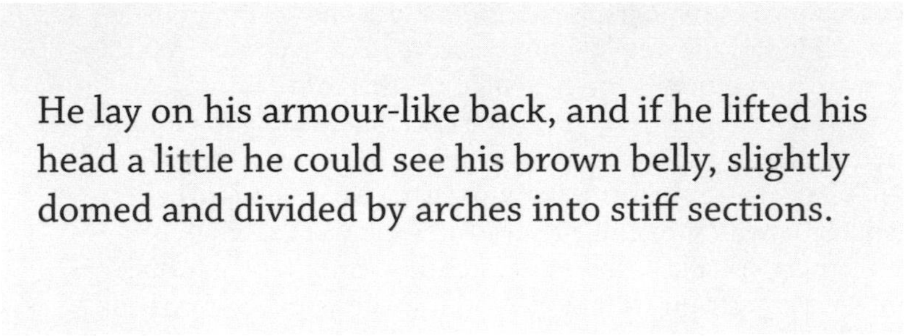

He lay on his armour-like back, and if he lifted his head a little he could see his brown belly, slightly domed and divided by arches into stiff sections.

FIG 1.1: A humble bit of text. But what actually happens when someone reads it?

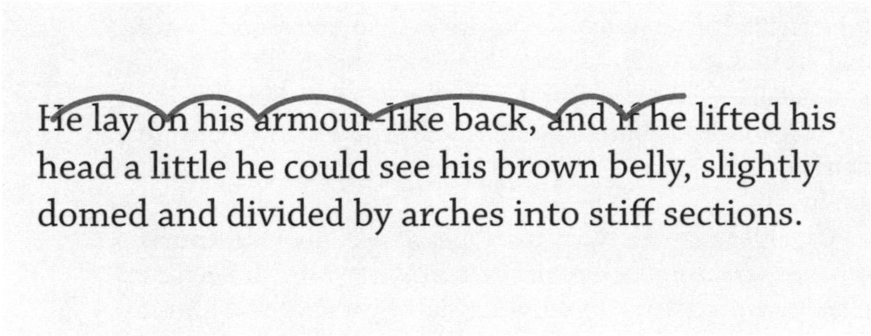

He lay on his armour-like back, and if he lifted his head a little he could see his brown belly, slightly domed and divided by arches into stiff sections.

FIG 1.2: Saccades are the leaps that happen in a split second as our eyes move across a line of text.

nd if h

FIG 1.3: Fixations are the brief moments of pause between saccades.

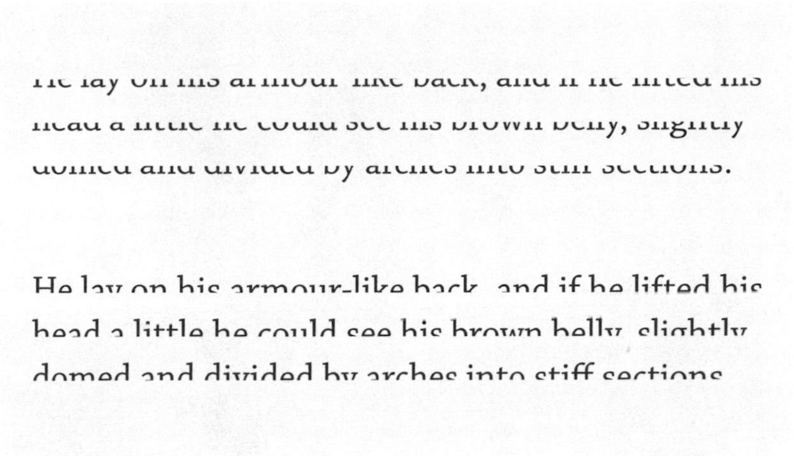

110 lay on his armour like back, and it he lifted his
head a little he could see his brown belly, slightly
domed and divided by arches into stiff sections.

He lay on his armour-like back, and if he lifted his
head a little he could see his brown belly, slightly
domed and divided by arches into stiff sections

FIG 1.4: Though the letters' lower halves are covered, the text is still mostly legible, because much of the critical visual information is in the tops of letters.

Between saccades, our eyes stop for a fraction of a second in what's called a *fixation* (**FIG 1.3**). During this brief pause we see a couple of characters clearly, and the rest of the text blurs out like ripples in a pond. Our brains assemble these fixations and decode the information at lightning speed. This all happens on reflex. Pretty neat, huh?

The shapes of letters and the shapes they make when combined into words and sentences can significantly affect our ability to decipher text. If we look at an average line of text and cover the top halves of the letters, it becomes very difficult to read. If we do the opposite and cover the bottom halves, we can still read the text without much effort (**FIG 1.4**).

This is because letters generally carry more of their identifying features in their top halves. The sum of each word's letterforms creates the word shapes we recognize when reading.

Once we start to subconsciously recognize letters and common words, we read faster. We become more proficient at reading under similar conditions, an idea best encapsulated by type designer Zuzana Licko: "Readers read best what they read most."

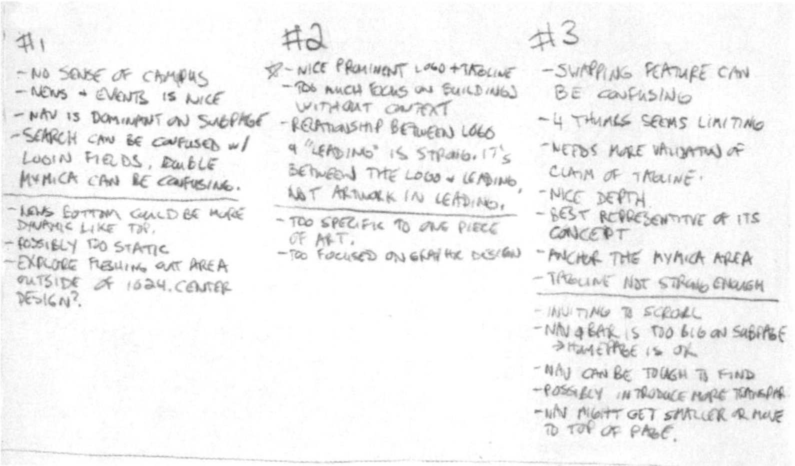

FIG 1.5: While you're very familiar with your own handwriting, reading someone else's (like mine!) can take some time to get used to.

It's not a hard and fast rule, but close. The more foreign the letterforms and information are to us, the more slowly we discern them. If we traveled back in time to the Middle Ages with a book typeset in a super-awesome sci-fi font, the folks from the past might have difficulty with it. But here in the future, we're adept at reading that stuff, all whilst flying around on hoverboards.

For the same reason, we sometimes have trouble deciphering someone else's handwriting: their letterforms and idiosyncrasies seem unusual to us. Yet we're pretty fast at reading our own handwriting (**FIG 1.5**).

There have been many studies on the reading process, with only a bit of consensus. Reading acuity depends on several factors, starting with the task the reader intends to accomplish. Some studies show that we read in *word shapes*—picture a chalk outline around an entire word—while others suggest we decode things letter by letter. Most findings agree that ease of reading

HE LAY ON HIS ARMOUR-LIKE BACK, AND IF
HE LIFTED HIS HEAD A LITTLE HE COULD SEE
HIS BROWN BELLY, SLIGHTLY DOMED AND
DIVIDED BY ARCHES INTO STIFF SECTIONS.

He lay on his armour-like back, and if he lifted his
head a little he could see his brown belly, slightly
domed and divided by arches into stiff sections.

FIG 1.6: Running text in all caps can be hard to read quickly when we're used to
sentence case.

relies on the visual feel and *precision* of the text's setting (how
much effort it takes to discern one letterform from another),
combined with the reader's own proficiency.

Consider a passage set in all capital letters (**FIG 1.6**). You can
become adept at reading almost anything, but most of us aren't
accustomed to reading lots of text in all caps. Compared to the
normal sentence-case text, the all-caps text feels pretty impen-
etrable. That's because the capital letters are blocky and don't
create much contrast between themselves and the whitespace
around them. The resulting word shapes are basically plain
rectangles (**FIG 1.7**).

Realizing that the choices we make in typefaces and typesetting have such an impact on the reader was eye-opening for me.
Small things like the size and spacing of type can add up to great
advantages for readers. When they don't notice those choices,
we've done our job. We've gotten out of their way and helped
them get closer to the information.

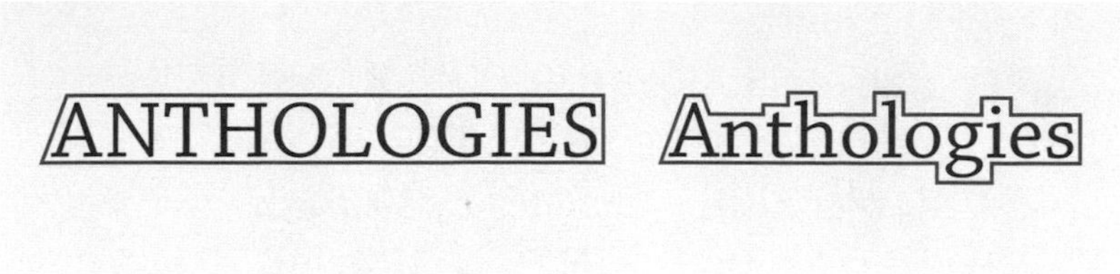

ANTHOLOGIES Anthologies

Anthologies

FIG 1.7: Our ability to recognize words is affected by the shapes they form. All-caps text forms blocky shapes with little distinction, while mixed-case text forms irregular shapes that help us better identify each word.

STACKING THE DECK

Typography on screen differs from print in a few key ways. Readers deal with two reading environments: the physical space (and its lighting) and the device. A reader may spend a sunny day at the park reading on their phone. Or perhaps they're in a dim room reading subtitles off their TV ten feet away. As designers, we have no control over any of this, and that can be frustrating. As much as I would love to go over to every reader's computer and fix their contrast and brightness settings, this is the hand we've been dealt.

The best solution to unknown unknowns is to make our typography perform as well as it can in all situations, regardless of screen size, connection, or potential lunar eclipse. We'll look at some methods for making typography as sturdy as possible later in this book.

It's up to us to keep the reading experience unencumbered. At the core of typography is our audience, our readers. As we look at the building blocks of typography, I want you to keep those readers in mind. Reading is something we do every day, but we can easily take it for granted. Slapping words on a page won't ensure good communication, just as mashing your hands across a piano won't make for a pleasant composition. The experience of reading and the effectiveness of our message are determined by both *what* we say and *how* we say it. Typography is the primary tool we use as designers and visual communicators to speak.

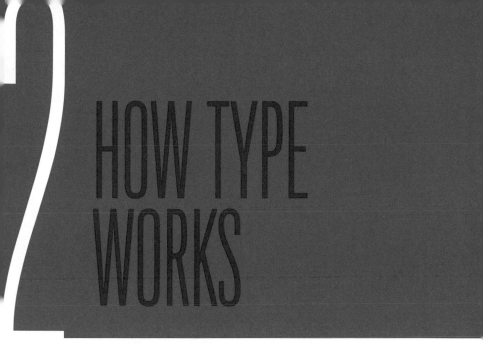

HOW TYPE WORKS

THERE ARE no rules in typography.

This is the hardest fact for people to grapple with when they try to familiarize themselves with the rules, because there aren't any. We have principles, best practices, and methods that work *most* of the time, but nothing that works *all* of the time. We can do our best to ensure that something is durable: good-sized type for reading, plenty of whitespace, pleasing typefaces, and visual appeal, but we can't account for all environments and devices, which are often in flux. Learning typography is about figuring out what choices work best for each situation.

Whether we're the designers or the readers, we're all part of the audience for those choices. From the moment we wake up to the time we go to bed, we're bombarded by type: newspapers and magazines, signs on subways and freeways, emails and web-sites, the myriad interfaces and labels adorning everything we touch. We're exposed to more type each day than at any other point in history. Type is pervasive—and thus so is typography—yet *bad* typography remains. Why?

Put plainly, good typography is hard. And the sheer number of options we have can feel overwhelming.

For one, more typefaces exist than any one person could use in a lifetime. Typeface families themselves are enormously intricate, some containing thousands of glyphs, and each of them containing many small details. Filtering through the options is a Sisyphean task. You also have to consider the elements of composition. Things like size, spacing, color, and tone all affect the reading experience.

The bulk of typography, if done well, isn't supposed to be noticed. Unlike a painting, song, or other creative output, type is a means, not an end. It's often said that good typography is invisible. Readers may only snap to the realization of the presence of type when they struggle with understanding what it's trying to convey. Namely: when typography fails.

When it comes to designing for the screen, we have even more considerations, from new devices with new screen resolutions every month, to techniques like responsive web design (http://bkaprt.com/owt/3/), let alone the constant temptation for visitors to click away from your site. With all these elements on the table, it's no wonder that many people find the prospect of using type a bit daunting.

But by creating websites, we assume the role of communicators. Whether you are a designer, writer, developer, or anyone contributing to a site, your work is connected to communication. Luckily, we have history on our side—many approaches to typography from centuries' worth of print design hold up on the web. We can stand on the shoulders of those who came before us. But first, let's dig deeper into typography's purpose.

WHY TYPOGRAPHY MATTERS

Whether online, in print, or on the side of a spaceship, typography is the primary vehicle we use as designers to communicate our message. When we get it right, it's powerful. And to do it well, we need to strike the balance between beauty and utility—and then disappear into the night.

Typography is one of your greatest design assets. It's not visual decoration or something that gets added at the end to spice up a design. Good typography gives spirit to words and is a potent mechanism to inform and delight.

It doesn't matter how well-considered your layout is, how wonderful your website's interactions, code, colors, imagery, or writing are. If your type is bad, the design fails.

Typography is communication

Most of the communicative heavy-lifting in our designs hinges on text. And because we're inundated with things asking for our attention, our typography needs to put its best foot forward. That means setting our type to avoid getting in our readers' way, and nudging them to give us a moment of their busy day. Through our typography, we're often politely asking: "Will you look at this?" With the glut of information out there, that question becomes a tricky proposition. Most people are short on time. By not caring, by not attending to your typography, you might as well close the browser window for them.

Through type, we're able to communicate our message and play with the tone and tenor of the delivery. Just as different musicians perform the same song differently, we can take a variety of approaches to the way we deliver a message.

With that in mind, you want to equip yourself with the best tools you can find, so you have the best shot at someone saying, "Yes! I want to read this!" Well, they likely won't say it out loud, but if you get them to stick around for a little while, that's just as good. You want to grab people and pique their interest.

AN EMBARRASSMENT OF RICHES

Given type's critical nature, it's no wonder we have so many typefaces to choose from. If you open the font menu in any application on your computer, you'll see quite a long list of fonts. Companies like Apple and Microsoft bundle fonts with their operating systems so you have a selection of basic options when you want to make something.

What's staggering to most people is how many fonts are out there. No one has an exact figure, but according to Karen Cheng, author of *Designing Type,* we have well over fifty thousand commercial typeface families out in the world, and even more free fonts and typefaces that never made the leap from the analog world of wood and metal type.

With that many fonts, you may ask why anyone would want to design new ones. Like the clothes we wear or the cars we drive, typefaces are a response to time, place, and culture. As our world and technologies change, so too must our means to communicate. New typefaces are welcome additions to our growing palette.

That said, we shouldn't leave behind some tried and true classics. While new typefaces have the ability to respond to technological advancements, old typefaces have design equity. Like a family legend that gets passed down through generations, they amass gravity and history. At times, these traditional typefaces capture a moment or feeling just by their presence. They're also a foundation for many new faces.

Until recently, the majority of typefaces were created for traditional printing processes. Type designers took factors into account like the thickness and texture of paper, how ink gets absorbed and dries, and the speed and physics with which printing happens. As an example, Matthew Carter designed Bell Centennial—a replacement for Chauncey H. Griffith's Bell Gothic—for AT&T with the printing of telephone books in mind.

Bell Centennial included a key design feature called *ink traps,* small notches cut into the tightest corners of letters to give ink a place to spread as it dries (**FIG 2.1**). At the time, telephone books were printed on newsprint, which tends to absorb and spread ink. The ink traps allowed the letters to expand to their intended shapes during the printing process. Without them, the letters would have been an over-inked blobby mess.

Carter's design was a response to the conditions the typography needed to withstand: high-speed printing with low-quality paper. These letters may look odd when you see them in their pre-printed form, but that's because they aren't finished until after printing. We don't need to accommodate ink traps on a digital screen, but we have plenty of other things to worry about.

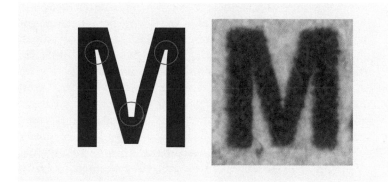

FIG 2.1: Bell Centennial has notches that fill with ink during printing to complete its letterforms. Without these ink traps, the tighter intersections would overfill as messy blobs.

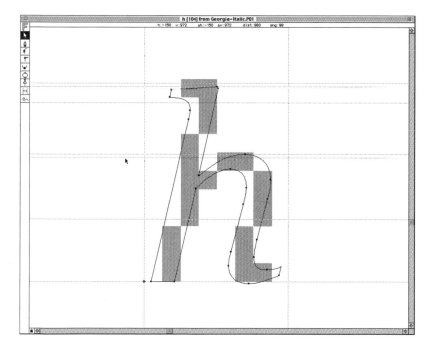

FIG 2.2: Georgia (pictured) and Verdana were designed as bitmaps first, outlines afterward. Image courtesy of Matthew Carter.

In the mid-1990s, Microsoft approached Carter to design typefaces for screen use. Verdana and Georgia are the most notable and lasting results of Carter's work. He started with bitmap fonts to match screen-rendering environments at the time. He then translated those forms into the smooth vectors that we know today as Verdana and Georgia (FIG 2.2). As he had with Bell Centennial, Carter optimized these typefaces for the current state of the medium, considering the attributes of the screen that affected their display. Both typefaces have a large lowercase height and ample spacing between letters to aid legibility. And while many designers may be a little tired of their pervasive presence, Verdana and Georgia remain among the most sturdy and realized workhorses for onscreen type ever made.

As display resolutions sharpen and rendering engines evolve, we need new typefaces that keep the conditions for screen-based media in mind. Visual communication on the web is growing up fast. Let's look at how far we've come.

TYPE ON THE WEB

We are just on the other side of a transitional state in typography. Until recently, if you wanted to get type onto a web page, you were limited to a few options.

System fonts

You could take the easiest route and tell a browser to use fonts installed on nearly every computer. Popular examples include Times, Verdana, Arial, and Georgia.

Images

You could load your typeface as an image, which freed you to use any typeface you had on your computer. The downside? The text was locked inside the image, which meant it was forever fixed at specific dimensions and resolution. And unless you took additional steps for accessibility, the text wouldn't be selectable, searchable, or translatable.

Text replacement

You could also programmatically hide text on a page with combinations of images, CSS, Flash, or JavaScript. Any hidden text was then replaced with an image or a pseudo-font file (e.g., a Flash file that contained the font's outlines). While these methods were more extensible than text images in some ways, they could feel foreign to readers, have mixed results with accessibility, and be difficult to maintain. In some cases, they even required additional technology (e.g., a Flash plugin).

Thankfully, all major browsers now support the CSS `@font-face` rule, which allows websites to link to font files like any other asset. Type foundries like Typotheque and Hoefler & Co. (formerly Hoefler & Frere-Jones) offer web licenses and hosting for their typefaces. Other companies like Typekit, Webtype, and Fontdeck offer subscription services with typefaces from various foundries. Specifying font files for your web pages is as easy as dropping a few lines of code into your CSS. For more on that, check out Paul Irish's article "Bulletproof @font-face Syntax" (http://bkaprt.com/owt/4/).

Loading fonts for use on a website isn't without its flaws. Like other assets, font files need to be loaded from a server, and they can be rather large. People aren't accustomed to waiting for every page asset to load just to serve up some text. But `@font-face` is easier, more accessible, and more future-proof than the old methods, and it's only getting better as font files get smaller and we develop better ways to handle the user experience while assets load.

Web typography has made huge strides in a short amount of time. We can now reliably use fonts outside of the handful of typefaces that are pre-installed on our readers' devices. CSS gives us more fine-tuned control over typography than ever before. We've broken away from less desirable, and sometimes inaccessible, methods like using images of actual font files. All of these changes mean we have better options for communicating in our designs. But as web practitioners, we not only need to be conversant in the technical side of designing for the web, but we also need to understand the visual nature of typefaces.

THE LANGUAGE OF TYPE

Half of the battle in understanding typography for the web or any other context is becoming familiar enough to talk about it. To know how to point out a serif or lowercase numeral. To be able to talk about the counters in letters or the kerning between them. As with other highly specialized skills, if you aren't the one who is ultimately responsible for bringing a design to fruition, you need to know enough to discuss it with the people who are. I may not know how to configure a server from scratch, but I know enough to have a conversation with an engineer about it. Being fluent in typography makes you part of the design process, and that's exactly where you want to be.

To develop your gut instinct for typography, start by learning the language of type. It will take your typography from mere words on a page to something that resonates. Learn what a descender and an ear are; recognize the differences between pixels, percentages, and ems when sizing type; know when to use small caps, an em dash, and more. Get the basic principles, or the stuff that works most of the time, under your belt and then take the leap on your own.

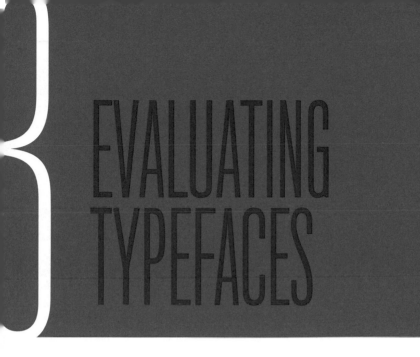

EVALUATING TYPEFACES

TYPE IS A TOOL. You need to understand the components of a typeface family to evaluate its potential. When it comes to designing for various screen sizes, internet connections, and browser capabilities, the importance of the decisions you make is compounded. Having a working knowledge of how a typeface fits into those considerations as a design asset will help you make decisions beyond what you see on the surface.

In this chapter, we'll look at some of the structural patterns in typefaces and see how they're grouped and sorted. Then, we'll examine what makes typefaces look the way they do from a visual and a technical perspective. But first, we need to talk about terminology.

FONT VERSUS TYPEFACE

Two common terms you'll see thrown around when talking about typography are *typeface* and *font*. *Typeface* is the name for the design in full, whether it's a style or family of styles.

For example, Helvetica is a typeface. Font refers to the format or storage mechanism for that design. `Helvetica.ttf` is a font. Typefaces can be made up of numerous font files. No matter how many files there are, it's still one typeface. Nick Sherman gave us a great analogy to remember the distinction: *a typeface is to a font as a song is to an mp3* (http://bkaprt.com/owt/5/).

How much does this distinction matter in day-to-day conversation? It depends on whom you ask. Most people use the two terms interchangeably. A friend might call me and ask, "What's a good font to use for the recipe I want to send my sister?" What they really mean is "typeface," but that's not the important thing here. The important thing is that *my friend is talking about typography.*

That's a huge step in getting people more comfortable with type! Does that mean you should let imperfect uses of "font" slide? Sometimes, yes. But since you know the difference between the two, you can also use it as an opportunity for teaching, *not* correcting (type lovers who spend the day swooning over typefaces have a hard enough time convincing others that we totally know how to party, thank you very much). Helping collaborators understand what's behind your choices lays the groundwork for better design discussions.

CLASSIFICATIONS

All typefaces fall into some sort of classification. Unlike the scientific organization of the animal kingdom, however, there has been little consensus on one scheme to rule them all. We struggle with these systems, because typefaces are thoroughly dynamic works diverse in visual structure, intent, influences, and historical context. Defining a classification system that comfortably accommodates typefaces from 500 years ago as well as five months ago—and getting everyone to agree on it—is not an enviable task. Fortunately, a foundation has settled enough for us to build on.

You're probably familiar with these classifications in a casual capacity. Groupings like *serif, sans serif,* and *script* are well known (**FIG 3.1**). More descriptive subclassifications exist to reference a particular set of physical traits or time periods. For instance,

Ag	Ag	**Ag**	*Ag*	𝔄𝔤
Sans serif	**Serif**	**Slab serif**	**Script**	**Blackletter**
Proxima Nova	Garamond	Clarendon	Bistro Script	Goudy Text

FIG 3.1: Examples of common typeface classifications.

some common subclassifications for serif are *Old Style* (e.g., Bembo) and *Modern* (e.g., Bodoni).

When thinking about typefaces for use in my designs, I mentally sort them into a few common groups: serif, sans serif, slab serif, script, monospace, and decorative (which is mostly made up of anything that doesn't fit into those other categories). Obviously, these groups don't represent all typefaces, but they work for the majority. Understanding the most basic classifications helps you filter the vast number of typefaces out there, and can be handy for searching on the web when you have a rough idea of the look or feel you're after.

While each classification evokes a kind of feeling, it's rarely something you can grab hold of because of how broad the classifications are. Two given typefaces may belong to the same class but spark very different responses, depending on their intended use or when they were made. Look to the typefaces themselves to support a feeling or mood in your design.

While not comprehensive, these working classifications help me sort typefaces against a mix of physical attributes and usage. For example, *decorative* isn't just a synonym for fancy type; it describes the context for using a typeface. A decorative typeface could have serifs or be a script or monospaced, but its overriding characteristics likely prevent it from everyday use.

Thinking of typefaces this way lets me slice my work into smaller chunks. If I'm designing a website that has articles, I'm generally looking at typefaces for running text. Most of what I'm after will fall in the serif and sans serif classifications, as typefaces in other groupings will be too distracting for long

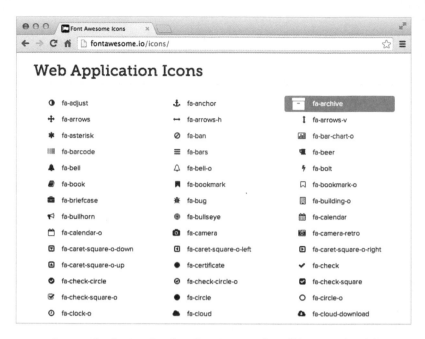

FIG 3.2: An example of an icon font from Font Awesome (http://bkaprt.com/owt/6/).

stretches of text. Along those lines, if I'm looking for a typeface to set my new tagline across the top of a website, I may look at more decorative or distinct typefaces first.

Beyond the traditional classifications, there is another category of typefaces: *icon fonts*. Icon fonts have characters filled with symbols other than letters (FIG 3.2). Pictograms in font form—also known as dingbat, symbol, picture, or pi fonts—have been around for a long time, but the urge to use them online is rising. There are clear, practical benefits: a scalable version of your logo or a shopping cart icon that you can size and color with CSS, while keeping the icons bundled as a single loaded asset. The benefits compound with responsive web design, since your icons can always scale up and down to the right size to suit a range of screens and resolutions.

But icon fonts can run into trouble online. Some of them remap individual letters to pictures, leaving little regard for someone using a screen reader, which may read the letter *e* aloud while displaying an icon of an envelope onscreen. For examples of icon fonts and best practices, check out Filament Group's handy article "Bulletproof Accessible Icon Fonts" (http://bkaprt. com/owt/7/). I have found, however, that the cons of icon fonts outweigh the pros, and I tend to agree with Chris Coyier and his article "Inline SVG vs Icon Fonts [Cagematch]" (http://bkaprt. com/owt/8/)—SVG is the more flexible solution.

Classifications, whether your own personal divisions or ones from an established system, can be a rabbit hole of information and history. And while they're interesting—especially when you want to geek out on type—you don't necessarily need to discern the minutiae of time periods and serif brackets to do your job. Classifications are helpful in the same way knowing about the history of jazz or rock 'n' roll can make you a better musician: they allow you to sort typefaces across criteria and find aesthetic and mental connections to help communicate your design. Sometimes these links are interesting juxtapositions or cultural references. Indra Kupferschmid covers classifications in detail and proposes a more flexible system for the future in "Type Classifications Are Useful, But the Common Ones Are Not" (http://bkaprt.com/owt/9/). Knowing about classifications makes you a better designer, because you can traverse these connections and use them to your advantage.

PHYSICAL TRAITS

Classification is only one facet of why a typeface may look and feel a certain way. But what causes some typefaces to appear larger than others when set at the same size? What causes them to feel lighter or heavier? And what makes the same letter look different from one typeface to another? The answers to these questions will help you understand the visual differences between typefaces. Understanding these traits lets you trace the varied ways typefaces approach and solve the same problems.

Typefaces are specialized tools, but they're also the expressive creation of a typeface designer. Some of the choices those designers make when creating a typeface may be based on a personal preference or technical reason. The sum of these choices

FIG 3.3: Some common parts of typeface anatomy.

influences the features we judge when choosing a typeface: legibility, flexibility, contrast, and more. Similar to classifications, a working knowledge of these traits gives you the power to speak confidently about typography—and helps you make mental connections between typefaces that share traits.

You're probably familiar with the basics of type: uppercase and lowercase letters, numbers, punctuation, and some special characters. Like any rich visual art form, typography has a vast depth of terminology to describe the diverse parts of letterforms. While you could fill another book discussing type anatomy—like Stephen Coles's *The Anatomy of Type: A Graphic Guide to 100 Typefaces*—I'd like to point out the most common parts of letters you'll encounter.

All letterforms are made up of a variety of *strokes*, a general term for most parts of a letter (**FIG 3.3**). Typefaces whose strokes vary in width to several degrees, from hairline thin to very broad, are known as *high-contrast*. Typefaces whose stroke widths are consistent throughout are *monoline* designs. Some strokes are straight and long, like the stem on a lowercase *h* or the descender on a *p,* while others are short and curved, like the neck and ear on a two-story *g.* Some strokes resolve in serifs, while others, as you sometimes see in the top hook of an *f,* can end in a bulbous shape as a *ball terminal* or a teardrop shape as a *lachrymal terminal.* Some strokes encase whitespace in what's called a *counter,* like the inside of an *o.*

Understanding the vocabulary of type helps you discover why a typeface looks the way it does, when or where it comes

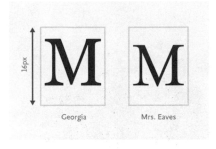

FIG 3.4: Two typefaces that appear to be different sizes despite being set to the same pixel size.

from, and its intended purpose. And greater knowledge of your tools means you're better equipped to make good decisions. Later in this chapter, we'll take a closer look at two familiar typefaces, Helvetica and Georgia, to see how we can extend this vocabulary to new typefaces.

In addition, a strong vocabulary for type is excellent when you're critiquing work. For instance, when you see inconsistent strokes or when something within a design feels off balance, you can point to a specific piece by name, rather than saying something like "that wiggly bit." That precision results in more productive discussions. For more information on why letters look the way they do, check out Tim Brown's article "Drawing Letters" (http://bkaprt.com/owt/10/).

EM BOX

Aside from the anatomical differences, typefaces also vary in physical size, and much of that variance depends on the relative size of the *em*. Despite the name, *em* does not refer to the size of the capital letter *M* in a given font. Rather, an em is a relative unit of measurement that's equal to your font size. So, if your text is set at 16 pixels, 1 em is equal to 16 pixels. This relative nature of the em is why it's so useful for responsive web design instead of fixed pixel measurements.

With ems, as far as the font is concerned, each character exists within a bounding box whose height is always 1 em (in this case, 16 pixels tall) but whose width varies (**FIG 3.4**).

FIG 3.5: Some metal type. The physical dimensions of the metal around the letter make up the em canvas.

That part is easy to grasp, but what many folks find troublesome is that the em is merely the *available height of each character's canvas,* and no rules state how much space a character can take up inside that box. We get this invisible box from a time when a type designer quite literally had a physical block upon which to design each letter—when fonts were tools made of metal and wood (**FIG 3.5**).

If you've ever set text in one font, changed it to another, and then noticed the text got smaller or larger even though you're using the same *numerical* font size, it's because of the difference in how large the glyphs were drawn in relation to the em (**FIG 3.6**). The font you switched to is designed to be smaller—a decision that resides with the type designer.

When it comes to web fonts, a type designer's intent has big implications for your design. Each web font you choose means a little more wait time for users as browsers load the font file. Some browsers handle that wait by displaying content as assets are still loading. When that happens, you may briefly see page content in a default font and then see it redrawn in the correct font when it's ready. The effect is a *FOUT,* or flash of unstyled text.

The more your web font veers in size or look from the browser's default font or your fallback font, the more noticeable the FOUT. The worst case is if your font fails to load entirely. If your layout depends heavily on the precise size of a font, it may break in unpredictable ways.

Anthologies

Georgia at 40px

Anthologies

Perpetua at 40px

FIG 3.6: Setting the same text in two separate fonts at the same `font-size` can result in two visually different sizes.

We do have methods to handle these issues, namely tools like Web Font Loader, which we'll look at later in this chapter. What's important to understand is that you need to consider the relative sizing of a typeface from a visual standpoint, not by numbers alone.

TYPEFACE CONTRAST

The *contrast* of a typeface refers to the differences in the thick and thin strokes of its characters. A monoline typeface has the absolute least amount of contrast. A typeface with low contrast has some, but relatively little, variation in the thickness of its strokes. For instance, Helvetica features consistent stroke widths. Compare that to a high-contrast typeface like Bodoni, whose strokes vary from beefy to delicate, all in one letter (**FIG 3.7**).

Higher-contrast typefaces tend to be useful in small bursts or headlines, because the extreme variation in stroke width is burdensome in long text. Our eyes are attracted to the exceptions— the stuff that looks different from everything else. Contrast is not only a duality of thicks and thins in the typeface, but it also involves the whitespace between and inside the letters. That variance adds up. I find I'm more likely to stop or slow down

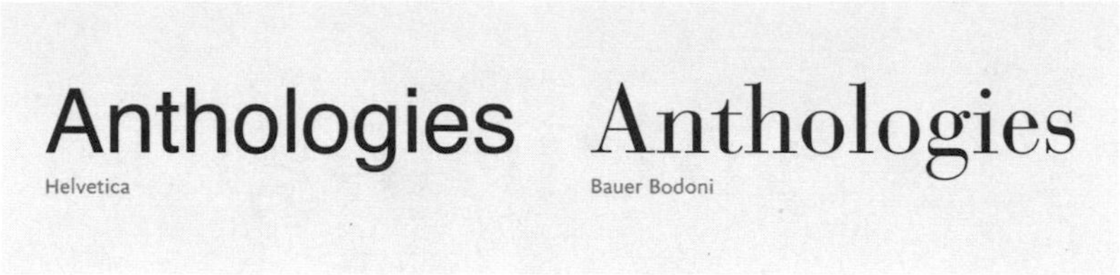

Anthologies   Anthologies

Helvetica   Bauer Bodoni

FIG 3.7: Two typefaces with differing contrasts.

and notice the letters, rather than read, when my eye encounters that kind of modulation.

A typeface with less contrast can create a smooth, welcoming rhythm for reading. Most typefaces intended for long-form text have medium to low contrast, which creates less interplay between the individual letters and words. This gives text a steadier visual rhythm as your eyes move across a line, which in turn aids readability. When we aren't distracted by the exceptions, we can focus on the act of reading itself. On the other hand, too little contrast in stroke or distinction between letterforms, as in the case of Helvetica, can be unsuitable for long stretches of text because the letterforms appear too uniform, reducing legibility. Like most things in design, it's about finding the right balance.

WEIGHTS AND STYLES

Many typeface families have at least four basic styles: *regular* (sometimes called *roman* or *book*), *italic, bold,* and *bold italic.* A style's *weight* refers to the thickness of its strokes, or their boldness. *Posture* refers to an alteration of the letter's skeleton, like the difference between regular and italic. However, variations in style aren't limited to weight and posture; they can include different optical sizes, numeral sets, and many other kinds of structural and stylistic alternates.

On the web, we commonly employ numerical CSS `font-weight` values. These currently range from 100 to 900—nine in total, each on the whole hundred value—with the lightest weight at 100 and the heaviest at 900. Not all fonts include every weight (some may only have a single weight), but this serves as

Bicycle
Bicycle
Bicycle
Bicycle
Bicycle
Bicycle
Bicycle

Bicycle
Bicycle
Bicycle
Bicycle
Bicycle
Bicycle
Bicycle

FIG 3.8: Some styles from the expansive Titling Gothic family.

a framework. While some typefaces deviate a little up or down the spectrum, most fonts place their normal or book weight at 400 and their bold at 700. Since these names and numbers aren't absolutely prescriptive, it's best to make your judgment visually to be certain you have the weight you want.

The four basics are a standard minimum set of family members, especially for text faces, but some typefaces are part of massive families. Take Titling Gothic by Font Bureau, the condensed sans serif used on the covers and chapter openings of the A Book Apart series. The style used for headlines is regular condensed, but it is only one of fifty-eight styles (!) that make up the Titling Gothic family. Family members range from very thin and condensed to very heavy and wide (FIG 3.8).

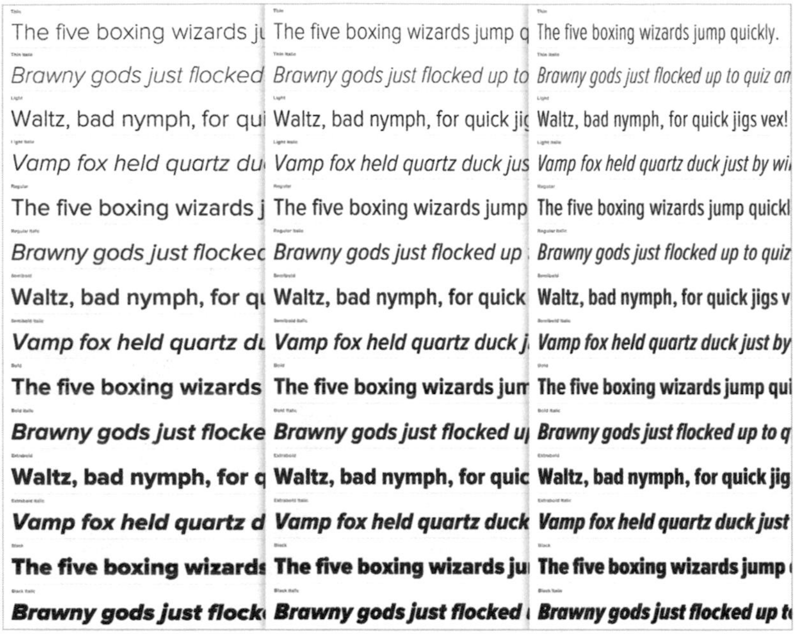

The five boxing wizards ju | The five boxing wizards jump q | The five boxing wizards jump quickly.

Brawny gods just flocked | Brawny gods just flocked up to | Brawny gods just flocked up to quiz an

Waltz, bad nymph, for qui | Waltz, bad nymph, for quick jig | Waltz, bad nymph, for quick jigs vex!

Vamp fox held quartz du | Vamp fox held quartz duck jus | Vamp fox held quartz duck just by wi

The five boxing wizards j | The five boxing wizards jump | The five boxing wizards jump quickl

Brawny gods just flocked | Brawny gods just flocked up | Brawny gods just flocked up to quiz

Waltz, bad nymph, for qu | Waltz, bad nymph, for quick | Waltz, bad nymph, for quick jigs v

Vamp fox held quartz du | Vamp fox held quartz duck j | Vamp fox held quartz duck just by

The five boxing wizards | The five boxing wizards jum | The five boxing wizards jump qui

Brawny gods just flocke | Brawny gods just flocked u | Brawny gods just flocked up to q

Waltz, bad nymph, for q | Waltz, bad nymph, for quic | Waltz, bad nymph, for quick jig

Vamp fox held quartz d | Vamp fox held quartz duck | Vamp fox held quartz duck just

The five boxing wizards | The five boxing wizards ju | The five boxing wizards jump

Brawny gods just flock | Brawny gods just flocked | Brawny gods just flocked up t

FIG 3.9: Proxima Nova, a very large type family by Mark Simonson.

Many families include condensed and expanded widths, which are what they sound like: *condensed* and *compressed* widths feature narrower letterforms, while *extended* and *expanded* ones have wider letterforms (FIG 3.9).

Why would anyone need so many styles? It depends on what you're designing. Flexibility is often one of my biggest considerations when choosing a typeface. If I can create a good level of contrast by using different styles within a typeface family, it accomplishes a few important things. For one, it lets me stay stylistically consistent within my design. I can use different styles for headlines, subheads, and maybe even text, and they will all share a common background throughout the piece. That flexibility helps me establish a clear hierarchy while keeping the visual language simple.

⚐ Bobulate

for INTENTIONAL ORGANIZATION

WRITING   WORK   WORDS   ABOUT   CONTACT

Evening edition

SEP 30, 2010   Long before the advent of a 24-hour workweek, before we were looking to multi-task (then to single-task), long before "getting things done" was a thing to get done, we got things done. On summer nights, the fireflies appeared and *"dinner's ready"* was a common call. On schooldays, the bell tolled. On television, the screen tuned out for the evening, static signaling the end of day. Signals, then, that signaled time shifting. Ends. Or more optimistic, beginnings.

Markerless time
Today, few markers mark time. We make our own markers, using light as a guide on some days, milestones and deadlines on more frenetic ones. But it's the rare person who, at 6PM, can walk, head high, out of the studio or office, turning day into night and one thing into another. Marking the fact that it's time to play.

Evening edition
The *Evening Edition* was always a signal. No matter what sort of news it delivered, it was a signal that even though what we were doing was important, the day was done, we should stop what we're doing and pay attention.

FIG 3.10: Liz Danzico's personal site uses a single type family but still achieves design diversity among different kinds of content (http://bkaprt.com/owt/11/).

I find that the more typefaces I use in a design, the weaker the design becomes. Many people say not to use more than one or two typefaces at the most. Though obviously not a rule, this can be a good guideline as it puts some constraints on your visual palette (**FIG 3.10**). Having a variety of typefaces can create a cacophony of mixed styles and messages. But when you work from a smaller pool of options, you allow yourself to rely on typographic attributes like size and color to create distinction. And those elements will naturally feel like they belong together, because they come from the same place.

Pay close attention to the members of a type family on the web, especially where browsers may try to fill in for a missing style. When text is set to bold or italic in CSS, the browser

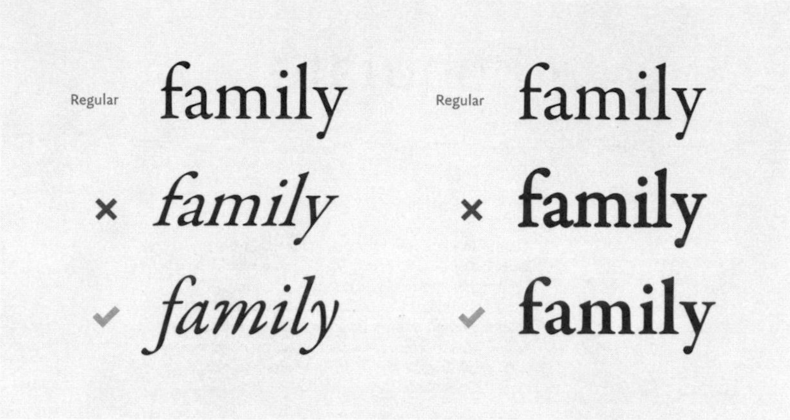

Regular **family**
× *family*
✓ *family*

Regular **family**
× **family**
✓ **family**

FIG 3.11: Comparing browser-generated pseudo italics and bolds with proper ones.

will first look for the appropriate font to render it. If that font is absent, the browser will try to formulate an italic or bold by artificially skewing or beefing up the letterforms from the existing font.

We call these *pseudo* or *faux* italics and bolds, and they're the typographic equivalent of mistakenly tucking your shirt into your underwear (FIG 3.11). Italics are not merely slanted letters, but instead have different shapes adapted from the typeface's normal upright style. Notice how the correct italic and bold seem tailored for their form? In this typeface, the italic letters develop a slant and some trailing strokes, and some letters change drastically, like the lowercase *a* morphing from a two-story to a one-story letter. Now look at the faux italic. It's literally a skewed version of the normal style. Some of the letters' thinner bits look squished, and the counters appear misshapen.

Moving to the faux bold, the letters are a bit blobby, like someone spilled water on paper and the ink started to bleed. The letters' serifs crowd together because the spacing wasn't created with these mutated letterforms in mind. Proper bold weights feel heavier than normal weights, but they may not have a uniform

FIG 3.12: Two typefaces with different x-heights.

increase in their body size. In this example, the correct bold is thicker in the areas that were already heavy, but the thinner strokes and serifs remain largely unchanged. Small details like this allow the visual weight of the typeface style to increase, but keep parts like counters from filling in. Choose typefaces that have the styles your text needs to display properly, or you will be laughed right off the web. Okay, maybe not, but it's an ugly misstep you can easily avoid.

X-HEIGHT

A typeface's *x-height* refers to the height of its lowercase letters from the baseline (the implied line that the letters rest on) to the top of an uppercase letter (**FIG 3.12**). Just as an em has little to do with the letter *M,* x-height does not specifically refer to the height of the lowercase *x.* But because we're talking about the height of lowercase letters, the two are usually equal.

Like the relative size of a typeface's body, the x-height can be as large or small as the type designer wishes. Some typefaces have very low x-heights, which can communicate elegance, as in the case of some script typefaces. A low x-height can also create an interesting tension between letterforms, as the contrast is more pronounced between upper and lower cases.

When considering text faces, a high x-height is usually ideal; more space for the letterform means more information to help the reader. This is true of typefaces for print or web, but is of utmost importance where interfaces or wayfinding are a concern.

FIG 3.13: As x-height increases, a typeface's letters can be confused. Image courtesy of Ralf Herrmann (http://bkaprt.com/owt/12/).

A typeface with healthy strokes and tall x-height can mean the difference between sparse text and one that fills out the space comfortably.

But a high x-height isn't always the winning choice. The larger the x-height in a text face, the less room for other distinctive characteristics. For example, the letters *a* and *d,* or *n* and *h,* can become difficult to distinguish as the x-height increases (**FIG 3.13**).

Just as important to readability are the spaces and openings inside the letters: counters and apertures. *Counters* are a letter's interior space. Counters can be enclosed, like the middle of the letter *o,* or open, like the middle of the letter *c.* An *aperture* is the actual opening of the counter, like the space between the ends of the letter *c.* Typefaces with a high x-height usually have large counters, and their letters take up more of the em box. That translates into more information as to what distinguishes a specific letter, but finding the proper x-height is a balancing act. While a higher x-height may mean larger space for counters and apertures, it's a tradeoff. Too big and you might diminish the recognizability of a letter. Too small and you might diminish the legibility of your text. Thankfully, we have a good deal of wiggle room. The easiest way to see if a typeface has the right mixture of attributes is to set some text and give it a read. If you get tripped up on some letters and letter combinations, it's probably best to keep looking.

Age 1234567890   Age 1234567890

Garamond Premier Pro with uppercase numerals   Garamond Premier Pro with lowercase numerals

FIG 3.14: Two numeral sets, with uppercase (left) and lowercase (right).

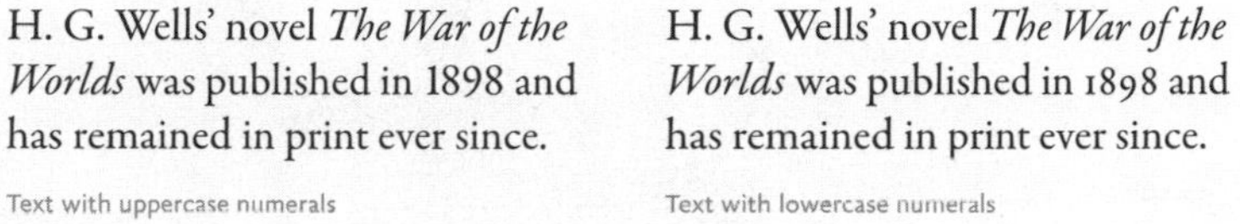

H. G. Wells' novel *The War of the Worlds* was published in 1898 and has remained in print ever since.

H. G. Wells' novel *The War of the Worlds* was published in 1898 and has remained in print ever since.

Text with uppercase numerals   Text with lowercase numerals

FIG 3.15: Uppercase numerals (left) can call too much attention to themselves in running text, but lowercase numerals (right) fit right in.

NUMBERS, PUNCTUATION, AND SPECIAL CHARACTERS

Strive to use typefaces that support numbers, correct punctuation, and special characters, especially if you're presenting your text in a variety of languages.

Numeral sets come in a few varieties (**FIG 3.14**). *Uppercase numerals* (sometimes also called *lining* or *titling figures*) have the same height and contrast as capital letters. *Lowercase numerals,* also known as *text* or *old style figures,* are designed for running text. Lowercase numerals act like lowercase letters, some with ascenders *(6, 8),* some with descenders *(3, 4, 5, 7, 9),* and some that reside at x-height *(0, 1, 2),* allowing them to blend in with text and cause less visual disruption than uppercase numerals. As you can see in **FIG 3.15**, uppercase numerals in text can call a lot of attention to themselves, while lowercase numerals continue the flow of text and read more evenly.

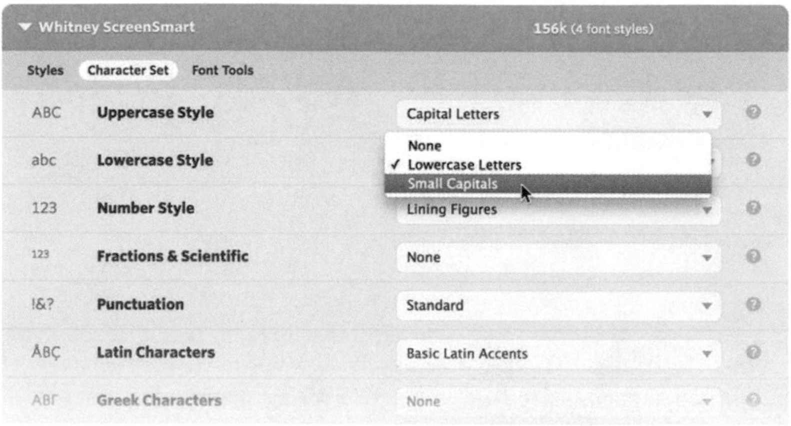

FIG 3.16: Hoefler & Co.'s custom configuration of fonts.

FIG 3.17: Tabular figures align vertically, making them easier to scan.

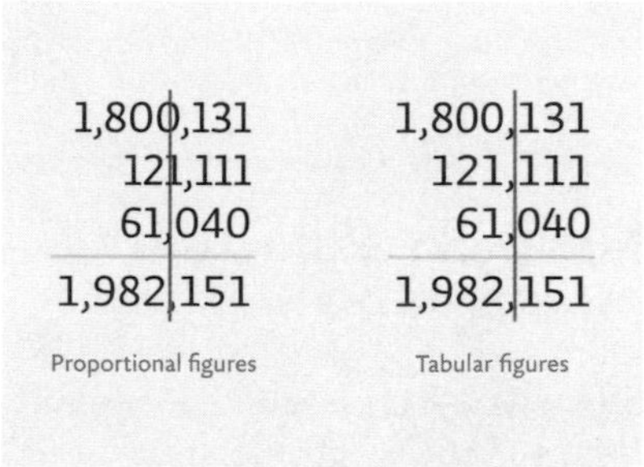

| Proportional figures | Tabular figures |

While many fonts might have only one numeral set, typefaces can contain multiple sets. This is sometimes a stylistic choice by the type designer—but it can also add to the size of your font files. If you're working with a typeface that has multiple numeral sets, you can access them with specific CSS rules for OpenType. Browser support for OpenType features is still gaining traction, but you can find a good browser-support matrix at CanIUse.com (http://bkaprt.com/owt/13/). Alternatively, some web font solutions, like Cloud.typography from Hoefler & Co. (http://bkaprt.com/owt/14/), let you select a numeral set or special character set to customize your font (**FIG 3.16**).

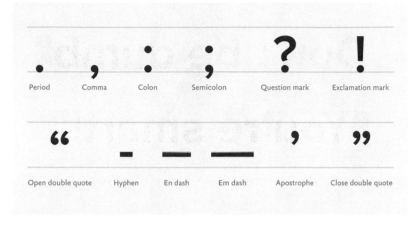

Period   Comma   Colon   Semicolon   Question mark   Exclamation mark

Open double quote   Hyphen   En dash   Em dash   Apostrophe   Close double quote

FIG 3.18: Some basic punctuation.

Tabular figures are numbers designed with fixed spacing for use in tables (**FIG 3.17**). Tabular figures keep your numbers lined up nicely in vertical columns, making data in things like tables and spreadsheets easier to scan.

For punctuation, make sure your fonts contain the basic forms you'll need for sentences (period, question mark, etc.), a set of dashes (hyphen, en dash, and em dash), and proper quotation marks (*not* straight quotes) (**FIG 3.18**).

Proper quotation marks are often overlooked, but it's important to know the difference. *Curly quotes,* usually called *smart quotes,* commonly look like filled-in 6s and 9s. *Straight quotes,* often called *dumb quotes,* are usually straight and vertical (**FIG 3.19**). Curly quotes are the correct punctuation for quoted text and dialogue. Dumb quotes are called as such because they are not only incorrect, but are also an instant sign of sloppy typography. Use of improper quotation marks shows a designer who either hasn't learned the right way to signify quoted text, or didn't spend enough time looking for a font with full punctuation support.

Punctuation is a system. That's why proper quotation marks and apostrophes look like they're part of the same family as

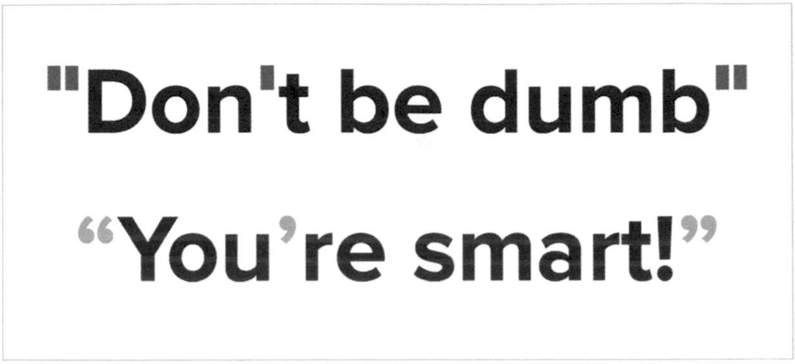

"Don't be dumb"

"You're smart!"

FIG 3.19: Proper quotation marks are usually curly or sloped.

commas, periods, colons, semicolons, and more, whereas straight quotes don't.

Straight quotes stem from the time of typewriters when keyboard real estate was at a premium, so reducing open and closing quotes to one key was economical. Unfortunately, this same choice of economy was copied to the computer keyboard and proliferated in the days of desktop publishing. Unless the software you're using corrects them, the default result when typing a quotation mark from your keyboard may be straight quotes. On the web, due to lazy implementations or force of habit, we're still plagued with dumb quotes.

Luckily, it's easier than ever to get proper quotes and apostrophes on your web pages, by either using the raw characters and specifying UTF-8 encoding or using HTML entities. Better still, use one of the many CMS plugins out there to automatically convert dumb quotes to proper quotation marks. Any of those methods is better than resorting to a claw-handed key combination to type them out.

I made a single-serving site called Smart Quotes for Smart People to show how easy it can be (http://bkaprt.com/owt/15/). For more info on quotes and dashes, check out Jessica Hische's excellent site Quotes and Accents (http://bkaprt.com/owt/16/).

"He was 6′4″ and full of muscle"

Feet and inches

40° 44′ 54.3588″ N, 73° 59′ 8.3616″ W

Latitude and longitude

FIG 3.20: Primes bear a resemblance to quotation and apostrophe marks, but are unique marks in their own right.

One last thing to note in the realm of quotation marks: *primes.* Primes look like italicized straight quotes and signify things like feet and inches, minutes and seconds, and coordinates on a map. Primes are not the same as dumb quotes; they're a different set of punctuation marks altogether (**FIG 3.20**).

It's not uncommon for free fonts to be incomplete or have mismatching punctuation. Most decent typefaces have the whole lot, but it's always a good idea to check before licensing a font or deciding to use a typeface.

SMALL CAPS AND LIGATURES

Some fonts contain alternate styles or characters like small caps and ligatures. *Small caps* are capital letters that are slightly taller than the x-height and often used for acronyms. It's important to note that these are not shrunken-down capital letters, but smaller capitals specifically designed to work alongside normal capital letters. Just as we saw with lowercase numerals, small caps have proportions that adapt the same stroke widths and contrasts in normal letters to maintain the text's visual flow. If you were to simply shrink down normal caps, the strokes would feel thin compared to the regular text, thus creating undue contrast (**FIG 3.21**).

✘ SHRUNKEN CAPITALS masquerading as small capitals

✔ TRUE SMALL CAPS blend perfectly with lowercase

FIG 3.21: Shrunken capital letters usually look too thin next to text, while real small capitals keep a consistent weight with the text.

FIG 3.22: Some letters commonly crash into each other, but this pitfall is easily avoided with ligatures.

Minion   Minion Pro

Using small caps on the web usually means specifying a separate font file with just the small caps. In some cases, the additional weight of another asset may deter you from using small caps, but it can really look stunning. Small caps aren't just an aesthetic decision, but aid readability by reducing the distraction of acronyms and other all-caps words in running text.

A *ligature* combines two or more characters to create a joined letterform. The most common ligatures solve for letterforms that unappealingly crash into each other. For example, in the *fi* ligature, the dot of the *i* would normally crash into the *f* and create a blobby mess. But by combining the letters, the dot of the *i* is removed and the top of the *f* extends over the base of the *i* (FIG 3.22).

Ligatures are useful in large text in which colliding letters create an unsavory disturbance, but they make running text feel smooth as well.

Web support for ligatures is getting better too. The CSS3 Fonts Module has several options for standard ligatures (such as *ff, fi, ffi*) and discretionary ligatures (*st, Th*), as well as options for small caps, text figures, and swashes (http://bkaprt.com/owt/17/).

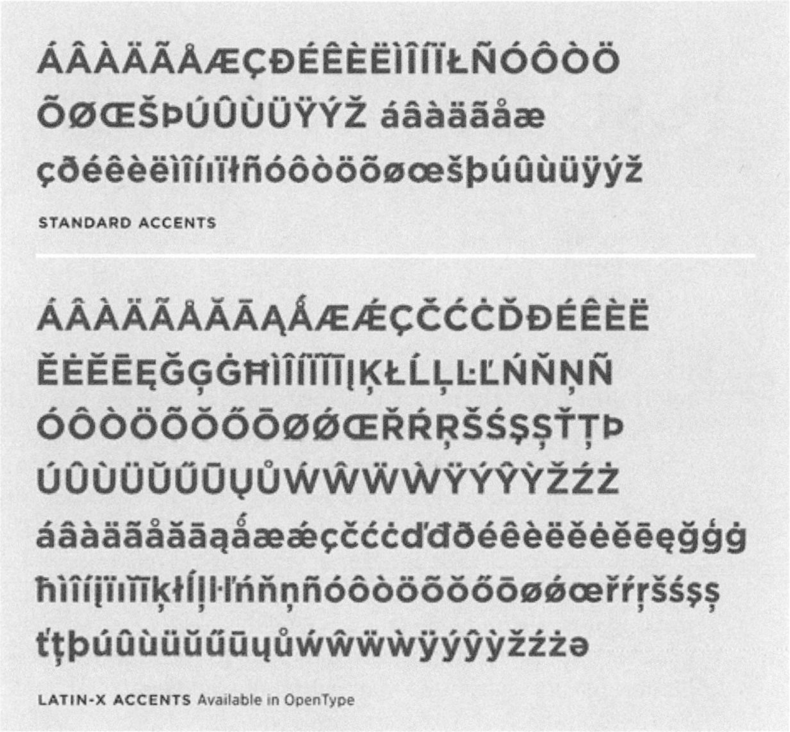

ÁÂÀÄÃÅÆÇÐÉÊÈËÌÎÏ˙ŁÑÓÔÒÖ
ÕØŒŠÞÚÛÙÜŸÝŽ áâàäãåæ
çðéêèëìîïïłñóôòöõøœšþúûùüÿýž

STANDARD ACCENTS

ÁÂÀÄÃĂĀĄÅÆÆÇČĆĊĎÐÉÊÈË
ĔĖĒĘĞĢĠĦÌÎÏĪĨĮĶŁĹĻĿĽŃÑŅÑ
ÓÔÒÖÕŎŐŌØǾŒŔŘŖŠŚŞŞŤŢÞ
ÚÛÙÜŬŰŪŲŮŴŴŴŴŸÝŶŸŽŹŻ
áâàäãăāąåæǽçčćċďđðéêèëĕėēęğġ
ħìîïīĩĩķłĺļŀľńňņñóôòöõŏőōøǿœŕřŗšśşş
ťţþúûùüŭűūųůẃŵẁẅÿýŷỳžźżə

LATIN-X ACCENTS Available in OpenType

FIG 3.23: Hoefler & Co.'s typeface Gotham with default accented characters and Latin-X
accents (http://bkaprt.com/owt/18/).

LANGUAGE SETS

Many professionally designed typefaces have the characters
you need to set text in dozens of languages. Even better, a massive and realized family like Hoefler & Co.'s Gotham, designed
by Tobias Frere-Jones, can support text in over 140 languages
(FIG 3.23).

Choosing typefaces that accommodate the languages you're
designing for is essential. When a browser needs to render a
word and your font doesn't support the needed characters, the
browser will cascade its way through your CSS font stack until it

résumé r□sum□

The word *résumé* is set in one font, but the accented *e* falls back to a default font or undefined character box.

reaches a font that does, or worse, it will display the *notdef* character: an empty rectangle. This happens most often with special and accented characters. Don't undercut your beautifully set type with odd characters in a system font. It's a careless mistake that you can easily avoid by researching your type choices and testing them in the browser. For this reason, it's good to ensure that your font stack is ordered as best as you can manage so that if fallback fonts are needed, you have a font that almost matches the web font you're using (**FIG 3.24**). Of course, this isn't always possible, especially with more decorative fonts. In those cases, it's best to make sure your font has what you need.

OPTICAL SIZES

Some typefaces have family members that suit a specific size range, called *optical sizes.* These variants harken back to the days of metal type, when different sizes of a typeface were cut independently to accommodate different sizes of output. For instance, an optical size intended for headlines was cut thinner than one for text, because it would be uncomfortably heavy if you just scaled the outlines up.

Most digital typefaces inspired by metal type are based on medium-sized fonts, so using them to set large type results in unbalanced and heavy typography. Similarly, using them to set small type results in crowded or harder-to-read typography. Type families like Adobe's Garamond Premier Pro are designed

The best text faces generally have some personality, but not so much that it distracts us from the content or experience of reading.

Garamond Premier Pro, Display

The best text faces generally have some personality, but not so much that it distracts us from the content or experience of reading.

Garamond Premier Pro, Regular

The best text faces generally have some personality, but not so much that it distracts us from the content or experience of reading.

Garamond Premier Pro, Caption

FIG 3.25: Optical variants are useful for making type look its best at a particular size range.

with alternate sizes like *caption, text,* and *display* (mostly meant for headlines) for this very purpose. Typefaces with optical sizes can be especially useful for screen typography, because you can pick tailored fonts for the size and output you wish to use (**FIG 3.25**).

Captions can get pretty small in print at around 6-8 points, but on the web, type that small would likely be illegible. On screen, captions work better at around 12 pixels, depending on the typeface you use and the environment it's rendered in. Some higher-resolution screens are more forgiving, because more pixels are devoted to rendering the text. We'll examine setting type at text and display sizes later in the book.

The rise of web fonts brings us more typefaces specifically designed for the medium of the screen. Font Bureau has released their Reading Edge series (http://bkaprt.com/owt/19/), a collection of typefaces "designed to function reliably at 9px-18px." Many of these families correspond to other existing optical styles. For instance, Benton Modern RE pairs with Benton Modern and Benton Modern Display.

Now that we have the vocabulary to talk about type, let's look at a few specific typefaces.

HISTORICAL CONTEXT

Just as we can pick typefaces suited to our intended output and content, we can also work with typefaces throughout history to piggyback on their historical connotations. Every typeface was created at a certain time and place; some were created with specific uses in mind or in response to the conditions of their use, as we saw with Bell Centennial. Even if a typeface is reminiscent of a time and place, looks can deceive. Remakes and revivals are common, like Hollywood movies—though revisiting typefaces usually yields far more pleasing results.

Classic typefaces

Even if you're not typographically inclined, you probably know the names of some popular typefaces, either by merit of having them on your computer or by hearing about them in public. Names like Helvetica, Garamond, Futura, Caslon, and Gotham may ring some bells.

Using "classic" typefaces can be a big time-saver, because they've generally proven themselves to be sturdy and inoffensive. But keep a couple of things in mind when considering a tried-and-true typeface:

Typography is inextricably tied to time. Styles come and go, and type fluctuates along with them. Many designs benefit from contemporary typefaces. Just because a typeface is classic or revered doesn't mean it has a place on a website. For instance, Caslon is a beautiful book face. Printers used to say, "When in doubt, use Caslon," because it was so dependable. But Caslon originated in the 1700s as a response to the low quality of paper and inks at the time. Those constraints don't exist on screen. As beautiful as it is, I have trouble recommending Caslon over more contemporary typefaces like Chaparral or FF Meta Serif, which better suit the screen.

Remakes and revivals

As you get more familiar with typefaces, you may start to notice variations or editions of the same typeface. In the same

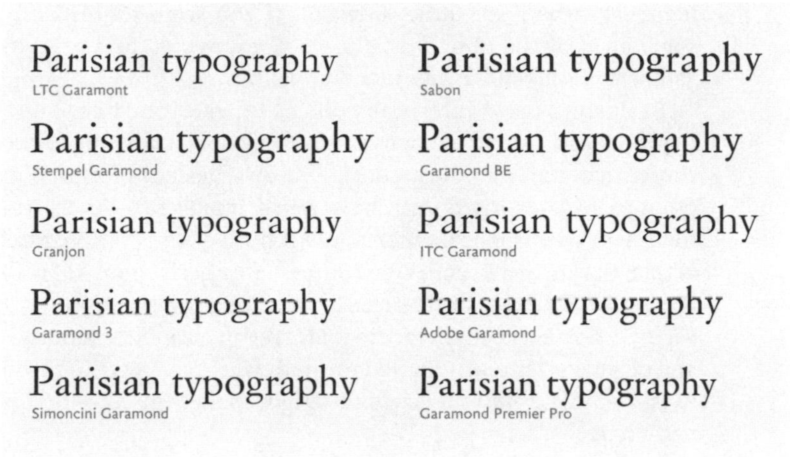

Parisian typography
LTC Garamont

Parisian typography
Sabon

Parisian typography
Stempel Garamond

Parisian typography
Garamond BE

Parisian typography
Granjon

Parisian typography
ITC Garamond

Parisian typography
Garamond 3

Parisian typography
Adobe Garamond

Parisian typography
Simoncini Garamond

Parisian typography
Garamond Premier Pro

FIG 3.26: A gaggle of Garamonds.

way popular songs make comebacks from time to time, so do typefaces. Because the original metal matrices or printings for these typefaces are often outside the realm of copyright, designers can revisit past works and digitally reinterpret them. As of this writing, more than a dozen versions of Garamond are out there (FIG 3.26).

Some of these Garamonds are based on the drawings and work of a 15th-century Italian printer named—you guessed it—Claude Garamond. Some Garamonds are based on the metal cuts of letters in Garamond's original work, while others are based on Jean Jannon's work that was misattributed to Garamond (http://bkaprt.com/owt/20/). Others are based on the phototypesetting fonts based on the metal cuts based on the original work. Still others are based on all of those things, with a bit of something extra thrown in. And on and on.

That doesn't even count the numerous Garamond revivals like Sabon, which seek to extend or sometimes "correct" earlier editions. How the hell can you determine which is the right one to use?

Each of these Garamonds is actually a different typeface. Some are technically better crafted than others; some are nearly identical; others are quite different. If you were set on using some form of Garamond on a project, you would first need to gather them up and evaluate their qualities.

Evaluating these interpretations can make your head spin. Do you judge a typeface based on how closely it adheres to the source material or in the context of its own design? Because I'm often more concerned with how well a typeface will perform than with its historical correctness, I prefer the latter. For example, Garamond Premier Pro (Robert Slimbach's 2005 revival) is based on different optical sizes of cast metal meant to support varied contexts. The typeface includes regular, caption, subhead, and display sizes, each crafted for optimal display within those uses. Such flexibility in size and weight makes this version especially versatile.

On the other hand, many designers consider ITC Garamond a particularly bad adaptation. Just ask Michael Beirut, who regretfully refused to read a book after discovering it was set in ITC Garamond (http://bkaprt.com/owt/21/). From its almost comically large x-height to the way some strokes seem to push and pull at odd angles, ITC Garamond may retain its namesake, but it takes enough liberties with the source material to reduce it to a mere Garamond-like substance. Its presence feels campy and retro in all the wrong ways.

Then we have Sabon (named for Jacques Sabon, a student of Claude Garamond), a Garamond revival that sought to modernize the classic design. Created by typographer Jan Tschichold, it was prominently featured in the design system that made Penguin Books famous. Sabon is a beautiful, flexible reinterpretation of Garamond. Its success is due in part to Tschichold's addition of italics based on the work of Robert Granjon, a Garamond contemporary. Tschichold designed the weights and styles to take up the same space when typeset so that compositors could use the same measurements to estimate the type fit, regardless of using regular, italics, or bolds. I bet Tschichold's collaborators threw him a parade for this wonderfully efficient solution.

Do you need to know all this information about Garamonds or any other typeface? Well, it pays to do your homework. It's one thing to choose a suitable typeface, but you can make a design even stronger by choosing one that matches the content *and* the context.

Revivals can be a mixed bag. They sometimes make great strides forward in design and in technical features for modern use. But they can just as easily make missteps, contorting the best parts of their predecessors. It's not always easy to tell the difference, but if you find a revival typeface you want to use, spend time reading up on its background. Getting well acquainted will make spotting a typeface's strengths and weaknesses seem like second nature.

FINDING ALTERNATIVES

The rewards of typographic knowledge are cumulative. If you already know a typeface well, you can build on that knowledge to find other typefaces. To do so, let's look at some specific visual attributes of a typeface. By scrutinizing a typeface, we can quickly determine if it suits our needs. Let's start with something we all recognize as an example: Helvetica.

Now, Helvetica is about as pervasive as a typeface gets; it's used on everything from logos to public signage around the globe. But is Helvetica the best choice for all of these uses? What are the visual attributes that make Helvetica *Helvetica* (**FIG 3.27**)? Let's take a closer look:

- Helvetica has very little stroke contrast; the lines are basically the same weight.
- It has a generous x-height.
- The letters are based on simple geometric forms.
- The apertures, or openings inside of the letters, are nearly closed. Helvetica hugs that space tightly.
- The terminals, or ends of the strokes, are at right angles.

From these attributes, we can deduce a few things: Helvetica is clear and geometric, but not always very legible. Since the letterforms carry so little variation, it can be easy to confuse some letterforms for others. If we need a typeface for small type or long-form content, we may need to keep looking.

FIG 3.27: A few physical attributes of Helvetica.

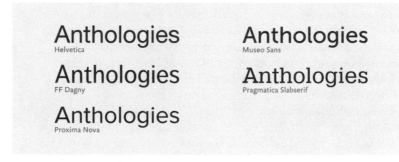

Anthologies
Helvetica

Anthologies
Museo Sans

Anthologies
FF Dagny

Anthologies
Pragmatica Slabserif

Anthologies
Proxima Nova

FIG 3.28: Some Helvetica alternatives.

Staunch devotees of Helvetica may decry any criticism of the typeface. Some people see it as the ultimate typeface for design, because it's basically a blank slate. They think you can throw anything at Helvetica and it will look just fine, because Helvetica brings little baggage and few connotations.

I feel the opposite. Helvetica is technically a beautiful face, but it's also so overused that I have trouble feeling any response when I see it. To me Helvetica has become a generic default. People use it as a safe choice rather than face the fear of making a bad choice. They'd rather say nothing than risk saying the wrong thing.

Take a stronger stance. Since we already broke down some of Helvetica's attributes, you can seek out typefaces that share similar traits (**FIG 3.28**). And don't worry if you aren't sure where to start looking—we'll cover some good resources for finding typefaces in the next chapter.

To start, let's look at FF Dagny. FF Dagny has similar proportions and counters, but it's slightly more compact without the perpendicular terminals. FF Dagny also feels more diminutive than Helvetica, and not so machined. Another option is Pragmatica Slabserif, which shares many of Helvetica's physical attributes but adds serifs, making it feel more academic. Either is a good option if you're familiar with Helvetica but want something a little different.

Let's try another example: Matthew Carter's darling of early web typography, Georgia. Used widely across the internet, Georgia is a modern workhorse for onscreen type. As we saw in the last chapter, Carter not only designed it for the screen, but he built Georgia to stand up to some of the least hospitable rendering environments. Can we find typefaces that embody that same durability but aren't as omnipresent? First, we need to break down what makes Georgia *Georgia* (**FIG 3.29**).

Let's take a closer look:

- Georgia features a moderate stroke contrast.
- It has a generous x-height, counters, and spacing across letters.
- It has some sharp and pointy angles, as if it were elbowing its way through a crowded room.
- It has beefy, almost slab-like serifs.

We gravitate toward a few key things. Due to its spacing, high x-height, and lower stroke contrast, Georgia is a great candidate for setting long swaths of text. And it's true: Georgia is a comfy typeface to sit back and read with. Because of the lower contrast, the letterforms carry a good rhythm, so text set in Georgia seems to flow. Georgia also has a mild heft to it—it's not quite a slab serif, but not a delicate flower either. With these traits in mind, we can track down typefaces that share similar attributes (**FIG 3.30**).

Take Chaparral (a personal favorite). It has some of the same traits that make Georgia so legible, like its x-height and openness, but with softer angles that evoke a more restrained elegance. Or

FIG 3.29: A few physical attributes of Georgia.

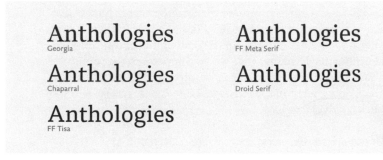

FIG 3.30: Some Georgia alternatives.

look at FF Tisa—a sure option for running text with more modern serifs and even less stroke contrast. Lastly, Droid Serif takes Georgia's angularity a step further as a pointier, boxier cousin, almost as if it's sucking in a small paunch to impress someone.

Comparing type like this is one of my favorite exercises because you can clearly see the lines between typefaces. We don't need to match every trait of a typeface we like to an alternate. The important thing is to recognize the traits that make the typeface unique. Playing off of that knowledge is extremely useful, because you can apply many of the same typographic methods as you would to the original typeface. Most important, building on that knowledge saves you time and makes you more proficient with type.

Now that you've learned how to look at and understand type's anatomy, let's see how we translate those traits to the screen, along with some considerations for bringing new assets to our websites.

TECHNICAL CONSIDERATIONS

Every typeface or typeface family consists of one or more font files. Fonts are individual files that contain the outlines of all the characters (i.e., the letters' actual shapes as vectors) and information from the designer to space and render the type.

Fonts are software. Chances are you've seen these files before. They're commonly TrueType (.ttf) or the newer standard, OpenType (.otf). OpenType fonts can contain outlines from either PostScript or TrueType fonts, but they're bundled in a common wrapper. OpenType fonts work for Mac and Windows systems, while older fonts and formats may only support one or the other. As a major bonus, OpenType fonts can support more characters, more languages, and special features, like small caps and ligatures, all in one file.

In 2009, the Web Open Font Format (.woff) was introduced to promote a single format that could work across all browsers. WOFF is essentially a wrapper that contains a TrueType or OpenType font, but significantly compresses the files for website visitors. These advantages make WOFF the best choice when it's available, and browser support is only increasing.

Loaded assets

All non-system web fonts are assets that need to download from a server for a page to render. While the trend is for file sizes to get smaller and connections to grow faster, you should keep the number of fonts you use to a minimum to keep your page weight as low as possible. Limiting your palette will help you maintain a coherent visual system and make sure your page load time is snappy.

Loading your fonts in CSS is the most basic way to get them onto your website, whether from your own server, a content delivery network (CDN), or a web font service. Depending on the size of your font file and the browser that's loading it, visitors may not see text in your font right away. They may see a page rendered in system fonts instead. But there are ways to orchestrate the loading process and have more control over what a visitor sees first.

Web Font Loader

Some browsers display content before all assets are loaded, while others wait until they have every asset to render the page. In the first case, a visitor will experience FOUT and briefly see content in a default system font before it snaps into the web font after the file loads.

A great way to deal with FOUT is by using Web Font Loader, a framework codeveloped by the engineers at Typekit and Google (http://bkaprt.com/owt/22/). It provides custom webhooks—callback events via CSS and JavaScript—so you can tell your page to use different CSS rules as fonts load, after they load, or if they fail to load.

Having more control is useful in a variety of circumstances. You could specify default fonts for your page and override those with web fonts after they load. Web Font Loader also lets you adjust sizes and styles before and after loading, so your page looks balanced in either scenario. For example, condensed fonts can take up less horizontal space and often need to be set a bit larger than other fonts at the same size.

Even if you're using Web Font Loader, you should still tailor your font stack to use the best fallback fonts for the situation. *Fallback fonts* are rendered when your web fonts fail to load, or are still loading. They're your best bet to having good typography shine through in your web fonts' absence.

Fallback fonts are the system fonts found on a visitor's device. Depending on the platform and operating system they're using, these fonts can vary. Code-wise, it's the same approach we've been using with CSS stacks for years, but with our web font added to the front, like so:

```
font-family: chaparral-pro, Georgia, "Times New »
Roman", Times, serif;
```

Here, I'm loading the font Chaparral with common serif system fonts as my fallbacks. Depending on the browser, the first fallback font may be used to render my design until Chaparral's file has loaded.

You can also use Web Font Loader to hide your content with the CSS attribute `display: none;` until your web fonts load, and thereby avoid FOUT altogether. But use caution: hiding your content also means a visitor won't see any text for a potentially long time, especially if your fonts have large files or take more than a few seconds to load. Further, if your web fonts don't load, content will stay hidden until your browser stops trying and times out, rendering the page in system fonts.

Some designers consider FOUT more of a feature than a bug, and I tend to agree. With reading and browsing happening on unknown connection speeds (like flaky cell connections), seeing content first can be a very good thing, even if it's not in your ideal typeface. The thing I try to avoid most in my designs is not FOUT but a jarring shift in the layout when a web font finishes loading. This shift is usually due to sizing discrepancies between your layout in system fonts and your chosen web font.

Because of these potential drawbacks, I prefer to approach web typography using system fonts (my fallback fonts) and save web fonts as a progressive visual enhancement partnered with Web Font Loader. This way, my pages load and render with nice typography even if JavaScript is disabled or some other unforeseen circumstance occurs. When the web fonts do load, Web Font Loader ensures that my CSS will switch over to the values appropriate for the fonts I'm using. But the fallback fonts are key. They're like the `alt` attribute for fonts, and they ensure that no matter what, your site can still be read.

With a little extra effort, you can use Web Font Loader to load your fonts asynchronously, or separately from the rest of the page and its assets. This means that if the files are large or slow to transfer, they won't block the page from displaying. Sean

McBride's article on the topic outlines a few different patterns, along with potential benefits and drawbacks (http://bkaprt.com/ owt/23/).

Rendering

Browsers and operating systems use a variety of technologies to display, or *render,* a font on a web page. As a result, a font can appear different in different situations. In some cases, a font that looks crisp and clear in one browser will look pixelated and ugly in another.

Fortunately, rendering problems like these are a temporary issue. Browsers are evolving and self-updating faster than ever, and as they do they're incorporating new, better rendering engines. Likewise, high-resolution screens—such as the Retina displays on the latest Apple devices—mean that some older rendering concerns are falling by the wayside.

That said, rendering quality is a factor we need to consider. Legacy browsers are still out there in large numbers, and they're often the worst affected. Even though rendering engines are improving, there are enough differences that we need to take them into account.

The two latest and best rendering engines are Core Text (used by Mac OS X and present on all iOS devices) and DirectWrite (used on the latest version of Windows). Both render text very well, but they do so very differently (http://bkaprt.com/owt/24/). Core Text adheres closer to the intended design, but it has a heavier hand with anti-aliasing that can make letters feel beefy or soft; DirectWrite, meanwhile, favors the screen's pixel grid, which can make the letterforms very crisp, but also spindly (**FIG 3.31**).

Neither approach is wrong; they're two ways to tackle the same problem. When people look at text on the opposite platform than they are used to, it can feel weird to them. When Safari for Windows introduced Core Text rendering to Windows users, many people were repulsed by the fuzzy text (http://bkaprt.com/ owt/25/). How we react to font rendering often comes down to what we're familiar with, not which approach is right.

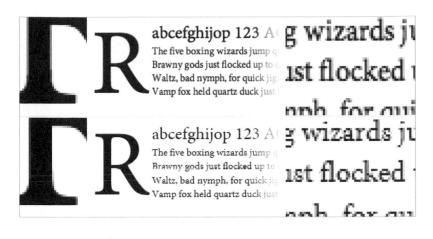

FIG 3.31: Examples of the same typeface and how it's rendered by Core Text (top) and DirectWrite (bottom).

With the level of fragmentation across platforms and devices, it's crucial to test our designs for proper typographic rendering and fidelity.

For more information on rendering type on the web, check out Tim Brown's articles, "CSS Properties That Affect Type Rendering" (http://bkaprt.com/owt/26/) and "Type Rendering on the Web" (http://bkaprt.com/owt/27/).

Soon, though never soon enough, rendering will be even less of a concern. Take heed, though; it still won't mean you can use any old typeface. But the conversation will shift toward appropriateness and technical acuity—that is, the *design*—and away from the display performance. For in-depth information about rendering and screen optimizing, see Peter Bil'ak's article "Font Hinting" (http://bkaprt.com/owt/28/).

We've gone through the gritty details on why typefaces look the way they do. Now, let's look at how to select and combine typefaces.

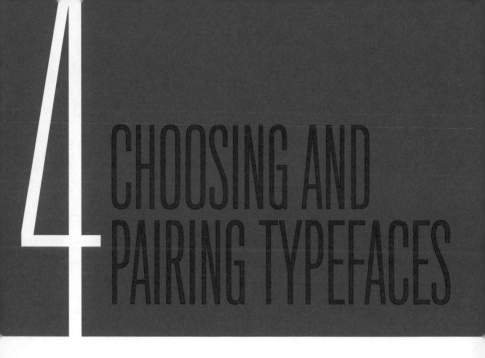

4 CHOOSING AND PAIRING TYPEFACES

ONCE YOU START down the road of looking at type as a tool and conveyance for communication, you turn into a new person: *someone who has opinions about type.* It's a dubious honor, and your friends will only tolerate you for so long as you sound off on the typefaces used on various restaurant menus. Your new excitement about type may also make you look like you have "answers," and we've already learned that that's a can of worms. As soon as you get that reputation among friends and family, they will inevitably ask you the same question: "What's a good font to use?" It's a difficult question, because typefaces don't exist in a vacuum. If you decided to make a painting, you probably wouldn't start by asking an artist friend, "What color should I use?"

Choosing typefaces relies on weighing the context of what you're designing against your technical requirements, typographic knowledge, and gut instinct. Just as the best coffee machine won't necessarily make you the best cup of coffee, good typography depends on the ingredients you choose, the particular combination of those ingredients, and the ways you combine them. Your typeface choices must fit the circumstances you need them for and so must your design.

And we're back to that old chestnut about rules: there are many right answers, and no answers are really *wrong;* there are just different degrees of *good.*

KNOW YOUR CONTEXT

As with any creative process, there are many approaches to choosing type, and it's a personal pursuit to find what works best for you and what feels most productive. But you have quantifiable considerations too, like the conditions under which you're going to use a typeface. I'm a minimalist by nature, so I like to simplify the kinds of uses for type into two camps: type for a moment and type to live with. Let me show you what I mean.

Type for a moment

Put simply, *type for a moment* is content that someone should only need a moment to read. This includes small interface copy (like a button or login link), brief asides to an article, and display type for a headline or large marketing copy (**FIG 4.1**).

As another example, think of it like a sign in an airport. It needs to quickly convey its meaning and let you be on your way. You don't want to spend precious minutes when you're late for a flight trying to decipher the artistic intent behind a sign before you can run off to your gate. And you don't want people to puzzle over where to click to find what they need.

After you get your readers' attention, there may be more to discover, like in the case of a logo or a big, promotional headline, but the key is to be clear up front.

The typeface you start with should suit a purpose. For navigation or interface text, I look for typefaces that hold up well at small sizes and aren't fussy with extra style. More times than not, I narrow it down to a simple sans serif. Let's look at JAF

FIG 4.1: An example of a big headline from FiftyThree's Pencil homepage (http://bkaprt.com/owt/29/).

Facit to see why. It can get very small, but it remains clear and legible because of its large, open counters and simple construction. Compare that with Futura or Zapfino (**FIG 4.2**). Either could work when used sparingly in a headline, but they both appear fussy as navigational text. They also take up more space. The strict simplicity of Futura's letterforms makes some letters hard to tell apart (for instance, the lowercase *a* and *o* look very similar), not to mention the tight spacing and small x-height. And Zapfino is a bit too decorative at the expense of legibility.

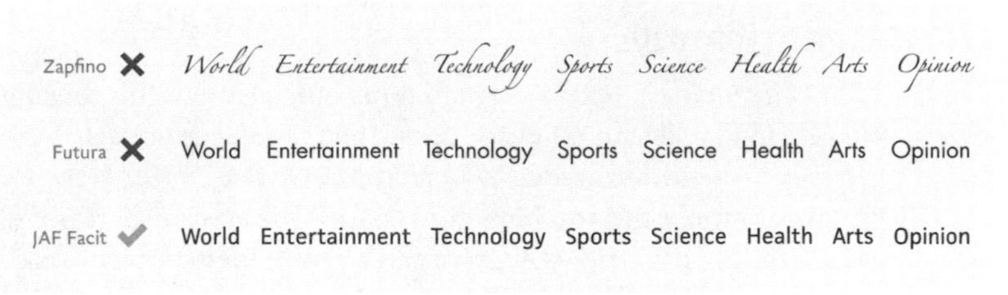

Zapfino ✘	World	Entertainment	Technology	Sports	Science	Health	Arts	Opinion
Futura ✘	World	Entertainment	Technology	Sports	Science	Health	Arts	Opinion
JAF Facit ✔	World	Entertainment	Technology	Sports	Science	Health	Arts	Opinion

FIG 4.2: JAF Facit versus Futura and Zapfino for navigational text.

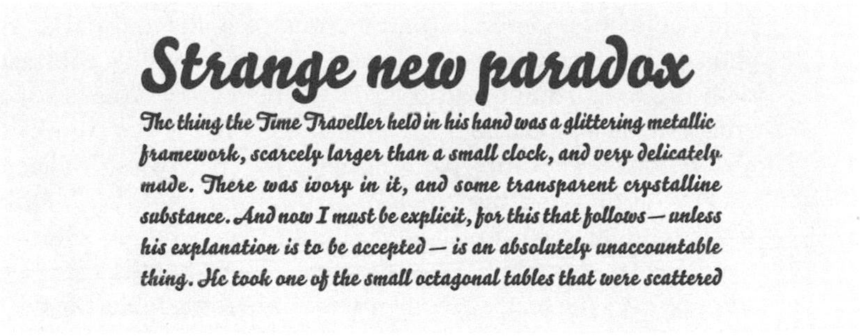

Strange new paradox

The thing the Time Traveller held in his hand was a glittering metallic framework, scarcely larger than a small clock, and very delicately made. There was ivory in it, and some transparent crystalline substance. And now I must be explicit, for this that follows — unless his explanation is to be accepted — is an absolutely unaccountable thing. He took one of the small octagonal tables that were scattered

FIG 4.3: Bello is beautiful, but not suited for longer text.

At larger sizes—especially in print or on a higher-resolution display—even delicate, light weights are easily readable. You can run the gamut of decorative typefaces and settings, as long as there isn't too much text. For extremely decorative headlines, stick to a few words or less. With these short bursts, type acts more like an image, so the viewer is more forgiving.

As you can see in **FIG 4.3**, using a decorative face like Bello for a headline doesn't give us much trouble as readers. A headline with a lot of personality immediately sets a mood, which can be a great way to draw a reader in. That said, you wouldn't want to use Bello for more than a line or two, as it quickly becomes cumbersome to read. Like salt, country music, and in-laws, a little goes a long way.

Type to live with

Type to live with is text we spend a lot more time with, usually long-form text like an article or book. The typefaces you use here can mean the difference between someone reading or not. If a typeface is too loud, too high contrast, or otherwise disruptive, we might lose the reader. And we can't blame them either—reading large swaths of text in all caps or in a decorative face is like yelling at a reader when you really mean to talk in an even tone.

Typefaces for longer reading should give a page an even texture. The texture of flowing text is the sum of the typeface's color (the general combinations of lights and darks in and around letters), the actual color of the text and its contrast with the background, and the size of the setting. You can see what I mean by blurring your eyes while looking at a chunk of text. If you see repeating patterns of weird letterforms that keep sticking out to you, the typeface may not be right. We'll look at typographic color in Chapter 6, but the general guideline is that a reader shouldn't notice the type. They shouldn't stop or stumble over the text, or wonder why something looks the way it does. Because when a reader notices the type, they're taken out of the act of reading and are instead trying to decode why something else is calling attention to itself.

In 1930, renowned typographic scholar Beatrice Warde penned an essay titled "The Crystal Goblet, or Printing Should Be Invisible" on this topic (http://bkaprt.com/owt/30/). She compares typographic choices to the difference between drinking wine from a clear crystal goblet—a vessel that lets you fully experience its contents visually alongside your other senses—or a goblet of "solid gold, wrought in the most exquisite patterns" that trades function for form. Warde urges designers to strive for clear presentation of their messages, allowing the contents to speak for themselves, and for designs to be a transparent window to those messages.

You want that clear goblet. Help people forget that they're staring at a screen and instead immerse them in the words and the story you're telling. The type you use should be smooth, removing as much friction as possible between the reader and the text (**FIG 4.4**).

Buster

Originally published in *Confrontation*, this story and seven more are available in *Facts About Blakey & Other Stories* from Amazon and Barnes & Noble.

"It's a confession booth," Jill says.

I stare at the large cardboard box in my sister's garage. A velvet curtain covers an opening in the box's side. "I thought I'd go to the party as *Visiting Brother*," I say.

"C'mon. I've spent all week on this costume. Try it on."

I put down my airline-tagged backpack. Over the velvet curtain, Jill has written *Confess Here, Sinner!* with a glitter pen. The box is surprisingly heavy. You could build homes from cardboard like this. The inside is perfumed shade.

"What was in here?"

"What?"

I part the curtain. "What was in here?"

"My new washing machine."

Behind Jill sits her Mercedes and a wall of plastic storage tubs. As for my sister, she looks the same as the last time we were together, a year or so ago. That is, radiant and healthy, as though California-born.

"It's stuffy," I say, taking off the costume.

"You'll love it, listening to people's secrets."

"Nobody is going to confess anything real."

"That reminds me. I have a non-disclosure agreement for you to sign."

I should mention that Jill is a lawyer, though she's probably kidding about the agreement. She draws up entertainment contracts or copyrights or something like that. A job like none other in my family. Serious money. Our father used to be a real estate agent. He sold plots of cattle land and stink-bad properties in Elgin. Mom was a substitute teacher for twenty years straight. Jill didn't want any of that. During semester breaks, she'd come home tan, pretty and wiser. She even sounded different, her voice completely free of drawl and bland as TV news. Sometimes I think she's adopted, gifted beyond our family's genes. It helps explain the alchemy of her success.

Jill hits a wall switch that brings down the garage door. I pick up my pack.

I've never been to a Hollywood party before. Nor Hollywood. My last New Year's party with Jill was a decade ago, back home. It was a mild Texas night and we ended up on the roof of our parents' home drinking, smoking and launching bottle rockets with our friends. My guys loved her friends because they were older, mostly girls, and pretended to be easily impressed. They were women, and we were boys. Jill's friends oohed and aahed whenever a bottle rocket reached the lowest of the clouds and burst inside with a warm glow. I remember my parents coming home from their

FIG 4.4: A nice space for reading from the site Stories and Novels (http://bkaprt.com/owt/31/).

The best text faces generally have
some personality, but not so much
that it distracts us from the content
or experience of reading.

Bree

The best text faces generally have
some personality, but not so much
that it distracts us from the content
or experience of reading.

Calluna

FIG 4.5: Calluna is simple, with just enough personality to make for an interesting text face. By contrast, Bree may have too much personality, making it potentially distracting for extended reading.

Choosing type for extended reading

When searching for good options for long-form text, we need to recognize that we're asking someone to live with this typeface for an extended period of time. Every eccentricity is amplified when used page after page. A visual quirk like a whimsical tail on the end of a *g*'s bowl may be cute when we see it once or twice, but over the course of a few pages, it can stick out and distract from the text, like that guy sitting in front of you at the movies whose nose whistles every time he breathes.

For instance, Bree is a beautiful typeface, but it also boasts a particular personality that I may or may not want in running text (FIG 4.5). Look at how some of the descenders (like the *g* or *y*) have a closed loop. It's a nice detail, but it plays cuter in text than I may want. These kinds of details shape the texture and overall mood of the page, much like how the tone or accent in a person's voice contributes to your impression of their speech.

In general, I've found it's best to look for typefaces that have a touch of personality (and I mean ever so little) and fulfill a few requirements. Like Bree, something with a big personality is appealing, but it runs the risk of overwhelming the text's message. When a typeface is decorative like a script or has embellishments like swashes, our eye is drawn to those exceptions. The smallest hint of idiosyncrasy—like extra contrast to the strokes or deeper descenders—adds some life to a text, especially since 99 percent of the type in the world seems to be set in Helvetica.

FIG 4.6: Three typefaces, ranging from small to large x-height.

Mrs. Eaves   Minion   FF Meta Serif

O O O

Omnes   Georgia   Bodoni

FIG 4.7: Three typefaces, ranging from low to high contrast.

Since a little personality goes a long way, it's useful to learn about the smaller details that set a typeface apart. Over the years, I've found myself looking at three main things when evaluating a typeface for extended reading: x-height, contrast, and letterforms.

Sufficient x-height

The lowercase letters should be tall enough to not feel dwarfed by the uppercase letters and create a nice balance at the page level (**FIG 4.6**). If the texture of the text looks like it favors the capitals too much, the x-height may be too small. Again, we're looking for features that will give us an even texture. In this example, Minion and FF Meta Serif are sufficient for most uses, but Mrs. Eaves may be too diminutive.

Low or medium contrast

A little contrast is okay, but too much can be, well, too much. In running text, a high-contrast typeface can really throw off the balance (**FIG 4.7**). In this example, the contrast on Georgia would work fine, but Bodoni may distract readers, and Omnes may prove too uniform as a result of its geometry. As we saw in Chapter 1, reading is easiest when we provide a smooth texture without too much contrast.

FIG 4.8: Some typefaces, like Gill Sans, have very little distinction among letterforms with similar structures. The *1*, lowercase *l*, and uppercase *I* blur together.

Gill Sans   Verdana

Recognizable and distinct letterforms

I shouldn't have to stop to discern if a capital *I* is a lowercase *l* or number *1* (**FIG 4.8**). Every moment I spend *decoding* text is a moment wasted. This isn't usually a problem in running text, where a reader has more context to help distinguish words. But it becomes paramount when a reader has fewer contextual cues, like a headline or a single word from an interface's navigation, or instances where numbers are mixed, like code, license plates, and serial numbers.

I keep these points in mind, because they can trip up readers. They're easy to temper once you know what to look for, but equally easy to get wrong if you don't take them into consideration when picking a typeface. Which brings us to...

METHODS FOR CHOOSING TYPEFACES

Below are a few exercises I work through as I plot out a design. One quick tip before we start: don't get attached. While you may have your list of the usual suspects, each project carries its own needs and goals. Be ready to abandon your favorite typeface. It doesn't matter if it's the loveliest hairline or the most elegant serif. If it doesn't serve your design, it doesn't serve the reader.

Word association

Selecting a typeface with that special something can be tough. With all the factors that go into a typeface, from aesthetic and historical nods, to the subtle effects of different kinds of serifs, how can you make a good choice?

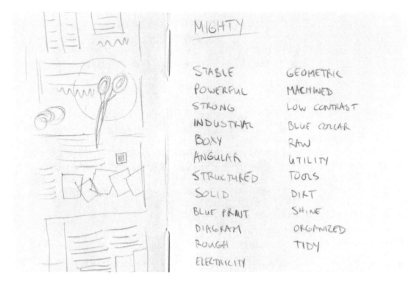

MIGHTY

STABLE	GEOMETRIC
POWERFUL	MACHINED
STRONG	LOW CONTRAST
INDUSTRIAL	BLUE COLLAR
BOXY	RAW
ANGULAR	UTILITY
STRUCTURED	TOOLS
SOLID	DIRT
BLUE PRINT	SHINE
DIAGRAM	ORGANIZED
ROUGH	TIDY
ELECTRICITY	

FIG 4.9: My list of word associations from early plans for the Mighty website design.

One method I use is word association. Rather than scrolling endlessly through pages of typefaces and getting tangled up thinking, "Is this the right one?", come at it from a different angle. Ask yourself: what do I want my design to convey? Think of words that describe the feelings or moods you'd like to impart. Perhaps you're designing a website for a day care. You may think of descriptive words like *playful, innocent, colorful, handmade,* and more.

Grab some paper and scribble down any words that come to mind. You're brainstorming, so there are no wrong answers, and you can always cross some out later. The important thing is to write as many ideas as you can. After you've exhausted that, start sorting similar words together into groups.

A while ago, I set out to design a quick page for my design consultancy, Mighty (http://bkaprt.com/owt/32/). I wanted the design to evoke feelings of being strong but casual. I wrote down words like *stable, powerful, industrial, boxy, angular, geometric, machined,* and *blue collar* (**FIG 4.9**).

ITC Franklin Gothic	**WE ARE MIGHTY**
Blackoak	**WE ARE MIGHTY**
Bree	**WE ARE MIGHTY**
Eurostile	**WE ARE MIGHTY**
Proxima Nova Extra Condensed	**WE ARE MIGHTY**

FIG 4.10: My shortlist of typefaces for the Mighty website design.

With these adjectives in hand, I can look for typefaces that suggest the same thing or help me portray those traits (**FIG 4.10**). For instance, to chase down the theme of *stable,* I may look at typefaces that run thick and strong. Blackoak is wide and chunky and looks like it could support a skyscraper.

This exercise breaks the process down into smaller pieces. Most important, word associations give you permission to delay answering that nebulous question, "Which typeface is right for my company?"—which can spiral into thoughts about what your company does, who works there, whom you work for, the building you occupy, and more. Those are key things to consider, of course, but they're larger ideas that the typography will come to support.

By narrowing your focus to a word or two, you may find it easier to collect potential typefaces. Once you gather a few contenders—and I'll share some of my favorite foundries and starting points later—it's far easier to address those other questions.

In the case of my company site, I chose a bold, condensed version of Proxima Nova and set it large in all caps (**FIG 4.11**). Though I was leaning toward Blackoak, it had some Wild West baggage. Eurostile had the right bones but felt too open,

WE ARE MIGHTY

Get Mighty

We all have a reason for showing up every day. Some do it for money. Others out of habit. At Mighty, we show up because we want to make stuff that matters. Simple things. Honest things. Beautiful things. Every day, we want to make things that affect people in positive ways.

↜ MIGHTY WORK ↝

Jason Santa Maria is founder of Mighty, a design studio. He houses his body of work at his **personal site**. He is a teacher, writer, speaker, AIGA board member, and overseer of all things Mighty.

© 2014 Mighty, LLC   Mighty on Twitter

FIG 4.11: The final Mighty homepage.

especially when compared with the way Proxima Nova seemed to stroll in and command as much of the space as it could muster. Its letterforms are simple and geometric without being bland. The final setting is powerful but not fussy, and fits the bill nicely. Proxima Nova's straight lines contrast perfectly with the Mighty logo's script lettering, adding some visual variety to an otherwise simple design.

Comparisons of real text

The most useful thing you can do when deciding whether to use a typeface is to try it out in a situation as close to the real thing as possible. If you're making a website, this means testing that typeface in context on an actual web page.

Some typefaces look beautiful when you see them in printed specimens or in the context of their marketing pages on type foundry websites. However, when you work with them in the frame of your own project, you may experience different results.

As we saw before, flourishes and pieces of letters may not seem like deal breakers, but then stick out in running text. In this regard, typefaces sometimes feel like "the clothes that words wear," as perfectly put by typeface designer Tobias Frere-Jones (http://bkaprt.com/owt/33/). If you've ever bought a pair of jeans that you thought looked great in the store only to find they look totally weird when you try them at home, you know what I mean. Typefaces need to be tried and tested in a real setting.

I often work up dummy pages that have little more than a few headings and paragraphs. It's basically a prototype, but I consider it more of a type sketch: not so refined as a design comp, but more revealing than browsing for fonts online. You can do this so quickly you have no reason not to. Simply drop blocks of the same text into an HTML document, set each paragraph to a different typeface or size, and open in a browser. Don't forget that typefaces can vary in appearance from one browser to another, so test a range of browsers and devices. Your typefaces should hold up across myriad environments.

Designer Richard Rutter made a template system for this express purpose called Body Text Tester (http://bkaprt.com/owt/34/). The web service Typecast (http://bkaprt.com/owt/35/) lets you test web fonts from a variety of foundries right in your browser, so you can play with the size and setting to your heart's content (**FIG 4.12**).

Many foundries and font services offer thirty-day trials or free plans so you can try some options before committing. Tools like FontShop's WebFonter (http://bkaprt.com/owt/36/) and Webtype's Font Swapper (http://bkaprt.com/owt/37/) allow you to preview any of their fonts on a given URL.

Once you review some typefaces in context, run through your list of aesthetic and technical requirements:

- Does the typeface have the right feel?
- Is it good for extended reading?
- Do the characters in your headline or company name look weird?
- Does the typeface family have additional styles you can use to flesh out your type palette?

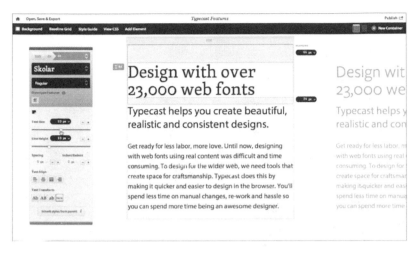

FIG 4.12: Informally setting type for some fast comparisons helps you identify or rule out potential picks. Typecast provides a quick means to try out type options in your browser.

At this point, I've ruled out a few typefaces and tucked the rest away for further experimentation. I may come out with two or three typefaces as starting points when I begin comping pages. There's no magic number—you may discover the perfect typeface and just roll with it—but this can be a valuable exercise to look at the possibilities from different viewpoints and whittle your options down to a chosen few.

Appropriateness

Just as we need to find typefaces that have the right stuff technically, we also need to ensure our choices are appropriate for our aesthetic context. Most of the time, it's not a matter of finding a singularly perfect typeface, but rather a matter of avoiding inappropriate ones.

As we've seen earlier, all typefaces stem from a specific time and place, and many have an intended purpose for existing. That purpose can be technical, as with Verdana, which was made for type on screens. Or it can be aesthetic, as with Trajan, which

FIG 4.13: New York's subway signage uses Helvetica almost exclusively.

was inspired by the chiseled letterforms of Trajan's Column in Rome. These qualities imbue your design with an air of a time and place; it's easy enough to conjure ancient Rome with Trajan. But these same associations can work against your design if they don't complement what you want to convey.

I live in New York and use the subway every day. Almost all of the signage for the subway system is set in Helvetica (http:// bkaprt.com/owt/38/). Helvetica is a Swiss typeface made in 1956 (the name *Helvetica* is based on the Latin name for Switzerland), and the subway design system was rebranded in the 1970s by Massimo Vignelli. So, it's a Swiss typeface in a design system made by an Italian designer for the American city of New York. The logical associations are scant, and I'd argue Helvetica is a bad choice. More important, as we saw in the last chapter, Helvetica's letterforms adhere to such similar geometry that it's difficult to discern one from another, making the typeface an even unlikelier choice for wayfinding signage (**FIG 4.13**).

FIG 4.14: The Freedom Tower cornerstone at the World Trade Center in New York uses Tobias Frere-Jones's Gotham, a typeface with roots in local signage (http://bkaprt.com/owt/39/). Photograph by Rick Mackler/Rangefinder/Globe Photos, Inc.

Compare that with the typeface chosen for the monument at the National September 11 Memorial & Museum. Both the identity and signage use Tobias Frere-Jones's Gotham (**FIG 4.14**). Gotham is a typeface born and bred in New York City. Not only is its designer from New York, but he took his inspiration from the city's indigenous typography as found in places like the Port Authority Bus Terminal. On the surface, this is a far more resonant choice, one that marries a typeface's origins to a project's meaning.

Of course, you could argue that Helvetica is a great choice for the New York subway, because it has become a worldwide design staple and New York is a melting pot of culture. And you may be right. As I said, there are no right answers, just different degrees of appropriateness.

How do we find out if a typeface is appropriate or, more likely, inappropriate? The best place to start is to track down information about the typeface itself, either on the designer's or foundry's website or in printed specimens. Like an artist's statement at a museum, a typeface's background information reflects the tremendous amount of thought and research poured into the work. Designers will often outline why they created a typeface, where they drew their inspiration from, what they intended the type to be used for, and more.

For instance, if you want to evoke a certain period, look for typefaces made during that time. They may not end up being what you need, but they have characteristics you can identify and use as criteria to find other choices.

It's hard to pin down cultural associations in typefaces, because they depend on the typeface's use in the wild. A great resource is the website Fonts In Use (http://bkaprt.com/owt/40/), which catalogs imagery of typefaces in real settings. The examples are well documented and tagged so you can quickly find work featuring a specific typeface. This is also a wonderful place to see which typefaces are paired with the ones you're researching.

A bit of research under your belt and attention to a typeface's connotations help make your design more cohesive. You'll also stand a better chance of avoiding bad typeface choices.

Avoid ready-mades

What's a *ready-made?* A typeface that has design baked in. These are the TV dinners of the design world: they (maybe) get the job done by doing the bare minimum. You see a lot of them around the holidays, such as spooky typefaces dripping in blood or dangling with icicles. Although those probably aren't for the *same* holiday.

Type choices like these limit you, because you can't escape the strong associations that come with them. They don't give you much room to work. Instead of using a font with design baked in, think about the associations you're trying to make. Remember, your typeface is the starting point, not the centerpiece. Let the *typography*—all of the ways you make that typeface be the voice of the message—do the talking.

Be careful with free fonts

Yes, fonts can be expensive, but that doesn't mean you should use free fonts either. We have a plethora of fonts at our fingertips, from scads of available foundries to our computers, which come bundled with a whole set. It's easy to take the amount of skill and time required to design a solid typeface for granted—and not just anybody can do it well.

A typical roman (meaning *upright*) face can take a type designer at least a year or two to complete. Depending on the design and designer, the size of the typeface family, the history and research involved, and the ebb and flow of the creative process, it's not unheard of for a typeface family to take five or more years to create. See Tal Leming, who spent over six years making his sans serif family Balto (http://bkaprt.com/owt/41/).

Beyond the basic set of Latin alphabet characters (*A-Z, a-z, 0-9,* common accented characters, and punctuation), a serious typeface family may include international character sets, multiple numeral sets, ligatures, small caps, and multiple styles for text, titling, and captions (**FIG 4.15**). That can add up to hundreds of individual glyphs per style, which means you're talking about potentially thousands of letterforms in total. That takes heaps of time, expertise, and testing, which you're less likely to get with free fonts.

In my experience, free fonts are a mixed bag and tend to suffer from common failings:

- Incomplete character sets (missing lowercase characters, or worse, punctuation)
- Less technical or aesthetic cohesion (the typeface feels uneven)
- A chance of being highly derivative of another font (sometimes due to an unaware or eager designer with good intentions)

Are free fonts doomed to failure? Not at all, but you should be extra cautious. Good fonts cost money because they take a lot of work to become good fonts. They can stretch your budget, but consider this: a type designer's work provides tools for us

a àáâãāăảäåǻăãǡąảǻâẩẫẩǎầẳẵẩẳắằặāāảặ

Lucida Grande

FIG 4.15: A small sampling of the accented characters you may find in a font with good multilingual support.

to use to make money, and our money gives them the means to keep making tools. We get paid for our work, and they get paid for their work. It's that simple.

Narrowing the field

One last way to make choosing type easier is to narrow the field from the get-go: create your own list of regulars. I keep lists of typefaces that I know well, or that I'd like to use, to give myself a head start when I sit down to work on a new project. Some are typefaces that've carried past projects; others I've come across and noted for future use when an opportunity pops up.

I've been asked what would top my list of "desert island" typefaces. Back in 2009, for the type-focused magazine *8 Faces*, I included typefaces like Caslon and Trade Gothic. A year later, when asked a similar question by FontShop, I had a few different choices like Garamond Premier Pro and News Gothic (http://bkaprt.com/owt/42/). My typeface shortlist changes every so often as various choices fall in and out of favor, or as I get to know others better, but I gravitate toward simple and sturdy sans serifs and book serifs.

As we saw in the last chapter with Helvetica and Georgia, your go-to typefaces serve as a springboard for finding new and related options. But you still need to cull the best typefaces for your design goals, which will shift with every job.

A great place to start is by referencing something whose design you already enjoy. Many books, magazines, and websites list their typefaces within the colophon for this purpose. For instance, in the back of this book, you'll see that A Book Apart uses FF Yoga and FF Yoga Sans for running text and captions, and Titling Gothic for condensed titles. If you like the way those typefaces look, you can try them out online and see if they work for your project.

If you see a typeface you want to learn about, you can use a bookmarklet like Fount (http://bkaprt.com/owt/43/) to reveal its name. You can also upload pictures to WhatTheFont (http://bkaprt.com/owt/44/) to find matches in MyFonts' extensive type database. Similarly, you can find typefaces with David Johnson-Davies's Identifont (http://bkaprt.com/owt/45/) by answering questions about the visual characteristics of different letters.

Or, maybe you're the kind of person who relies on recommendations or scours new typeface releases. Sites like I Love Typography (http://bkaprt.com/owt/46/) cover type releases on a regular basis, and many textbooks and design annuals offer beautiful examples that identify the typefaces used.

When I started out, I learned a lot by following in the footsteps of designers whose work I admired. People like Jan Tshichold and his wonderful work at Penguin Books, Fred Woodward and his eclectic editorial design for Rolling Stone in the late '80s and '90s, and, of course, Paul Rand and his amazing branding and identity systems. I tried similar combinations of typefaces they used to better understand how the typefaces functioned. Work from these and other designers served as a treasure map to typographic gold. Finding designers you like and adopting their type palettes can be a great way to build your own library.

As you become more familiar with typefaces, you may start to favor a handful of foundries. There are some foundries whose work I follow very closely, because they consistently produce great stuff that both speaks to me as a designer and is useful to the kind of design work I do. Some of my favorites are Mark Simonson Studio (fantastic revivals and, of course, Proxima Nova), Tim Ahrens and Shoko Mugikura's Just Another Foundry (wonderful text faces), Font Bureau (amazing book and display types, and some of the best web fonts around through Webtype), and Darden Studio (lovely text and display faces, with italics that flow beautifully). With so many more foundries to love! See a longer list of my favorites in the Resources in the back of this book.

Phew, where were we?

You've got oodles of ways to approach choosing an appropriate typeface. But what happens when you need more than one?

METHODS FOR PAIRING

Pairing typefaces gives our designs more variety, and it makes it much easier to create hierarchy and contrast, so we can group similar types of information (e.g., headings, sidebars) under a common visual system and guide the reader around our websites.

One or two typefaces are enough for most designs. When in doubt, a good rule of thumb is to pair a serif and a sans serif. This provides you with what are likely the two most flexible kinds of typefaces, and nearly guarantees you have sufficient variation between the two as they're inherently different. Obviously, this method doesn't ensure a *good* pairing, but it should help you avoid a bad one.

When it comes to choosing and pairing typefaces, I keep two things in mind: *distinction* and *harmony*. To keep the system you've created for visual communication properly balanced, you need to choose typefaces that don't compete too much with each other, but aren't so similar as to be indistinguishable. For instance, I would avoid pairing two serifs like Caslon and Baskerville, because they share too many traits (**FIG 4.16**). Placing them in the same design wouldn't yield any advantage, as most people wouldn't be able to tell them apart. I'd be better off using one typeface, or, better yet, choosing a contrasting sans serif like Museo Sans.

It's a tricky balance to pinpoint something that's different *and* complementary, but we can achieve that by flexing what we've learned about the structure of letterforms, like stroke contrast and x-height.

Look for distinction

Creating distinction can be as simple as pairing typefaces with strong visual differences, as in the case of a decorative script like Bello and an angular sans serif like Auto (both designed

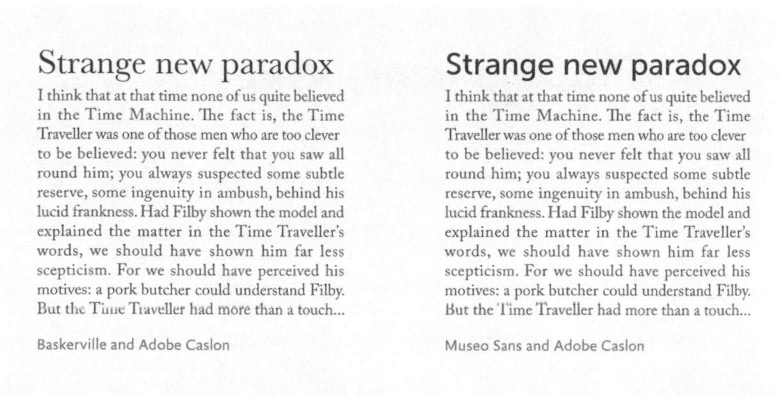

Strange new paradox

I think that at that time none of us quite believed in the Time Machine. The fact is, the Time Traveller was one of those men who are too clever to be believed: you never felt that you saw all round him; you always suspected some subtle reserve, some ingenuity in ambush, behind his lucid frankness. Had Filby shown the model and explained the matter in the Time Traveller's words, we should have shown him far less scepticism. For we should have perceived his motives: a pork butcher could understand Filby. But the Time Traveller had more than a touch...

Baskerville and Adobe Caslon

Strange new paradox

I think that at that time none of us quite believed in the Time Machine. The fact is, the Time Traveller was one of those men who are too clever to be believed: you never felt that you saw all round him; you always suspected some subtle reserve, some ingenuity in ambush, behind his lucid frankness. Had Filby shown the model and explained the matter in the Time Traveller's words, we should have shown him far less scepticism. For we should have perceived his motives: a pork butcher could understand Filby. But the Time Traveller had more than a touch...

Museo Sans and Adobe Caslon

FIG 4.16: Baskerville and Caslon are too similar and are easily confused when used together, but Museo Sans provides a nice contrast.

by Underware). Both are solid typefaces—nice aesthetics, full character sets, stylistic alternates, and OpenType features—and their visual contrast results in an interesting push and pull. Bello is like the eccentric friend in a road trip movie, while Auto is like the protagonist trying to get from point A to point B (**FIG 4.17**).

But the distinction need not be so pronounced. You can keep it subtle and still get the job done. Extending this example, you could pair stalwart Auto with a lower contrast or sturdier serif like Chaparral for a bookish departure. Although they're built on similar bones—both feature straightforward, non-decorative letterforms—they're still different type styles (sans serif versus serif), so they work well together (**FIG 4.18**).

If you do play it more subtly, be sure you have enough distinction between your two choices to make it work. In general, it can be difficult to pair typefaces that share a lot of traits. Don't be too subtle. For instance, I usually avoid pairing two sans serifs or pairing two serifs together, because of the lack of distinction. Without enough contrast, the hierarchy is less clear, and we want to reinforce our design system whenever possible. Using typefaces that are too similar muddies that up.

You can also achieve distinction in the way you employ your typefaces. A strong type system with distinct sizes, styles, and

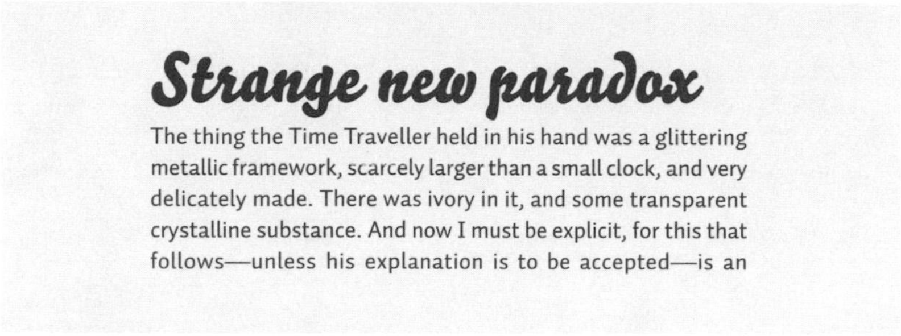

Strange new paradox

The thing the Time Traveller held in his hand was a glittering metallic framework, scarcely larger than a small clock, and very delicately made. There was ivory in it, and some transparent crystalline substance. And now I must be explicit, for this that follows—unless his explanation is to be accepted—is an

FIG 4.17: Bello and Auto make a good pairing.

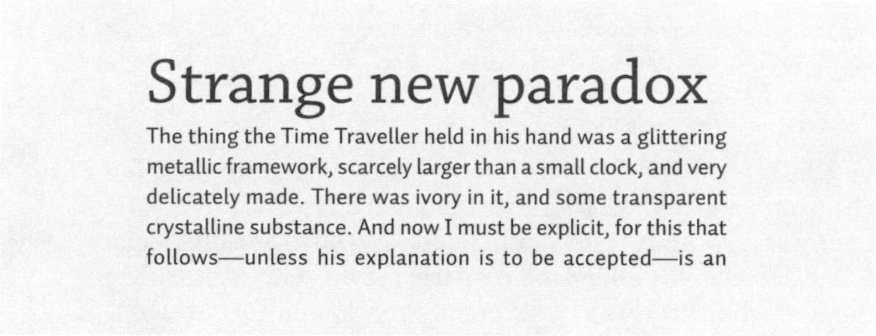

Strange new paradox

The thing the Time Traveller held in his hand was a glittering metallic framework, scarcely larger than a small clock, and very delicately made. There was ivory in it, and some transparent crystalline substance. And now I must be explicit, for this that follows—unless his explanation is to be accepted—is an

FIG 4.18: Chaparral and Auto make for a cozy, bookish feel.

usage for specific kinds of content gets you the most mileage. (We'll look closer at systems for typographic design in the next two chapters.) Visual changes like letter-spaced all caps, italics, bolds, condensed weights, colors, and combinations thereof make a diverse palette for your type, even within a lone typeface.

For example, on the latest version of my personal website, I use only Chaparral and a couple widths of Proxima Nova (**FIG 4.19**). But by playing with the sizes and colors of particular elements, I've established a typographic system. Even though I only use two type families, the different elements on the page feel distinct and stand on their own.

FIG 4.19: My personal website uses only two typefaces, but still feels like it uses a rich typographic palette by playing with size, spacing, and color (http://bkaprt.com/owt/47/).

Look for harmony

Typographic harmony comes from a combination of things: size, hierarchy, layout, color, juxtaposition, and anything else that affects the visual presentation of information. A good way to build a foundation for harmony is by finding typefaces with inherent visual relationships in their structure. Complementary forms strengthen connections between typefaces and, in turn, your design. For instance, many typefaces have similar skeletons or strong geometrical foundations based on circles and rectangles. Find two typefaces that share similar shapes, like Helvetica

Bauer Bodoni # The Time Machine

Helvetica Neue # The Time Machine

FIG 4.20: Same skeleton, different body. Helvetica and Bodoni pair well together, because they share similar underlying geometry but differ in contrast.

FIG 4.21: Joanna and Gill Sans were both made by Eric Gill and share a very similar skeleton.

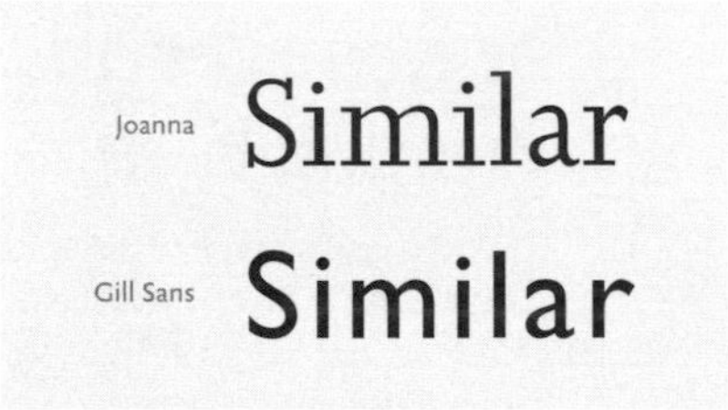

Joanna # Similar

Gill Sans # Similar

and Bodoni, and pair them together. Then they can play off of each other. Their shared skeletons form a visual union, but their contrasting letterforms spark healthy dissonance (**FIG 4.20**).

Harmony is based on both visual structure and gut instinct, but if you're stuck, one reliable method is to work with typefaces designed with systems in mind, like superfamilies. These systems commonly have a serif and sans serif counterpart meant to be used together.

Returning to the A Book Apart series as an example, I used FF Yoga and FF Yoga Sans by Xavier Dupré for the running text. Dupré designed these typefaces to complement each other, so they work nicely right out of the box. Both faces have the same basic structure but diverge beyond that, with one a nice book serif and the other a pleasingly low-contrast sans serif.

As another approach, opt for typefaces that share the same maker. Take Joanna and Gill Sans by Eric Gill (**FIG 4.21**). Just

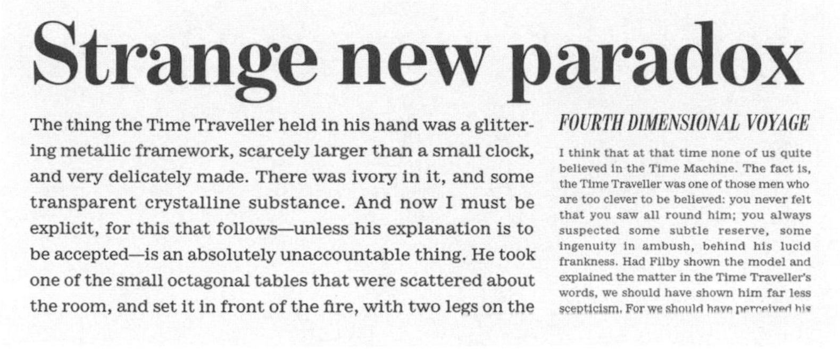

Strange new paradox

The thing the Time Traveller held in his hand was a glittering metallic framework, scarcely larger than a small clock, and very delicately made. There was ivory in it, and some transparent crystalline substance. And now I must be explicit, for this that follows—unless his explanation is to be accepted—is an absolutely unaccountable thing. He took one of the small octagonal tables that were scattered about the room, and set it in front of the fire, with two legs on the

FIG 4.22: One typeface, the expansive Benton Modern family, readily supports a diverse typographic palette.

as you can hear a new song by a favorite band and have it feel familiar, you can see the designer's hand in these two faces.

You can simplify things further by staying within a family that has a variety of styles. For instance, a large family like Benton Modern gives you lots of options for establishing hierarchy by varying the weights or widths of different elements (**FIG 4.22**). I wouldn't recommend using *all* of the weights from a large family, but two or three are enough to give you a broad palette to work with. Here, I use Benton's display weights for the headings—including a condensed style for the sidebar—and Benton Modern RE for the copy, a text weight tailored for small sizes.

Start with one and build outward

The easiest way to tackle combining typefaces is to lock in one typeface choice and build on it. Remember how we pulled Helvetica apart to see how and why it looks the way it does? You can apply that same exercise to any typeface to find another one that would make a good companion.

For example, let's say our top pick is Proxima Nova, a crisp, geometric sans serif. It has low stroke contrast, is a touch wide, and is more than a little round. That's our starting point. From there, we can choose fonts with qualities that either juxtapose

STRANGE NEW PARADOX

The thing the Time Traveller held in his hand was a glittering metallic framework, scarcely larger than a small clock, and very delicately made. There was ivory in it, and some transparent crystalline substance. And now I must be explicit, for this that follows—unless his explanation is to be accepted—is an absolutely unaccountable thing. He took one of the small octagonal tables that were scattered about the room, and set it in front of the fire, with two legs on the hearthrug. On this table he placed the

Fourth dimensional voyage

I think that at that time none of us quite believed in the Time Machine. The fact is, the Time Traveller was one of those men who are too clever to be believed: you never felt that you saw all round him; you always suspected some subtle reserve, some ingenuity in ambush, behind his lucid frankness. Had Filby shown the model and explained the matter in the Time Traveller's words, we should have shown him far less scepticism. For we should have perceived his motives: a pork butcher

FIG 4.23: Proxima Nova and Abril contrast nicely.

Strange new paradox

The thing the Time Traveller held in his hand was a glittering metallic framework, scarcely larger than a small clock, and very delicately made. There was ivory in it, and some transparent crystalline substance. And now I must be explicit, for this that follows—unless his explanation is to be accepted—is an absolutely unaccountable thing. He took one of the small octagonal tables that were scattered about the room, and set it in front of the fire, with two legs on the hearthrug. On this table he placed the

FOURTH DIMENSIONAL VOYAGE

I think that at that time none of us quite believed in the Time Machine. The fact is, the Time Traveller was one of those men who are too clever to be believed: you never felt that you saw all round him; you always suspected some subtle reserve, some ingenuity in ambush, behind his lucid frankness. Had Filby shown the model and explained the matter in the Time Traveller's words, we should have shown him far less scepticism. For we should have perceived his motives: a pork butcher could

FIG 4.24: Pairing Proxima Nova and FF Meta Serif feels modern and friendly.

or complement those features. We may decide to play off of Proxima Nova's linear strokes and generous width by pairing it with Abril, a high-contrast serif that's a bit condensed (**FIG 4.23**). The simple openness of Proxima Nova pleasantly combines with Abril's quiet austerity.

Alternatively, we could complement Proxima Nova's uniform strokes with a low-contrast serif like FF Meta Serif. Both fonts are very clear and legible and feature a high x-height—so we have a lot of flexibility for text or display typesetting with this pairing (**FIG 4.24**). Proxima Nova feels modern and friendly set large as headlines, and FF Meta Serif adds a wonderful bookish quality to the text.

You can see how breaking down a typeface's components helps you identify opportunities to create harmony or dissonance for the sake of your design system.

FIND YOUR OWN CLASSICS

To sum up, you have many avenues for choosing and pairing typefaces. It pays to be a design sponge in the world, so take note of what works and keep refining your visual palette. I pore over editorial design magazines and newspapers, because I love the way text looks in long form. I also love digging into well-designed books that deeply consider the reading experience; I discovered one of my favorite text faces, Fred Smeijer's FF Quadraat, by first seeing it in a book a friend was designing. (I'm pretty sure it was about mythical beasts. Or Batman.) Inspiration can hit when you least expect it.

Traditional printing, like posters and letterpress, also inspires and informs the way I design. Something about the constraint of a few colors or typefaces creates beautiful opportunities. I hoard posters and books, and take every chance I can to get the letterpress clanking.

Finding the kind of typographic design that speaks to you helps you spot your own influences and develop your own canon of design classics. To be an informed student of typography, you need to train your brain to look for good typography everywhere. This is actually easier than it sounds. Once you're aware of type, you can't help but notice the good and (unfortunately) the awful. But this is one of the parts of typography I enjoy most: we always have new methods and tools to discover at every turn, because typography is a living craft. We're all standing on each other's shoulders, pushing this rich tradition forward.

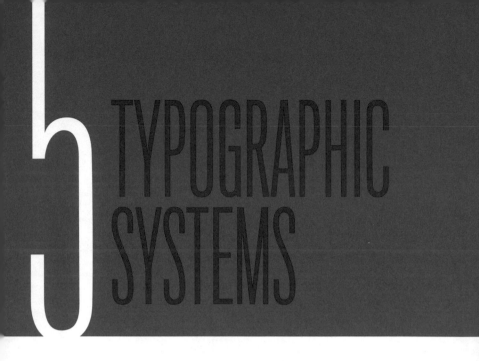

5 TYPOGRAPHIC SYSTEMS

TYPOGRAPHY IS an art of finding and shaping relationships between elements, from largest to smallest and smallest to largest. Now that you understand the technical and aesthetic sides of evaluating typefaces, let's zoom out a little more and talk about how typography's smaller building blocks come together as a communication system. In the next two chapters, we'll explore how content elements within a design affect one another and how the nature of the medium itself shapes our designs.

Like any good system, typography provides a method to accomplish a task. A typographic system establishes *hierarchy*, meaning it helps us prioritize content based on individual elements and relationships between them. It also helps our readers easily scan chunks of information and understand what they're looking at. When done right, a typographic system feels intuitive, like an unspoken set of instructions. Without any internal logic in place, our content may look like a monolithic block, essentially stranding readers in a dark room without so much as a match.

Luckily, we have some powerful tools at our disposal to help our typography form a strong foundation. And some of our most potent tools are also our most basic: size, space, color, and proximity. Together, they give us an infinite number of possibilities for crafting our messages in effective, readable ways.

HIERARCHY AND CONTRAST

On the surface, hierarchy may seem like a simple visual translation in which the most important items are the biggest and the least important are the smallest, but it's far more nuanced than that.

Size is one way to achieve hierarchy, but you could also do so with color or placement; the real heavy lifting happens when you combine two or more of these properties. The most important things don't always have to be the largest; they just need to be more distinguished than other elements. In other words, they need more *contrast*.

Contrast is, in my humble opinion, the most crucial tenet of graphic design. It instantly forges connections and distinctions between elements and, when used in concert with other tools like a grid, it helps our viewers discern what's vital, what's related, and what's not. That information gives readers the ability to navigate our designs efficiently. Without contrast, everything on a page may appear similar in size and importance, leaving a viewer the choice of either reading and decoding every bit of information or bouncing away to look at adorable cat GIFs.

A new order

Hierarchy applies a systemic approach to grouping similar items and distinguishing dissimilar ones. We express hierarchy both semantically (in the underlying HTML markup) and visually (in our design). For instance, if you look at the default browser stylings for things like an h1 or a paragraph, you'll see a baked-in hierarchy: h1s are bigger than h2s and h3s, and are distinct from a paragraph's style.

The best way to create a hierarchical typographic system is to first audit your website's basic elements. You can break down these elements in a variety of ways. Sometimes it's based on what the elements are semantically, as with headlines like h1 and h2 and so on; other times it's based on what those elements need to do, as in the case of very small type like captions or specialized text like block quotes. Understanding the subtle distinctions helps you make your type more readable and efficient—and ensures that your type suits an element's purpose.

One more note: since hierarchy is a system, be sure to keep it consistent. For instance, you may determine that headings and subheadings are always red and all caps, with supplementary text (like captions) set in Georgia at 12 pixels with a color of #666. Whatever you decide, once you've established those traits, deviating from the rules for similar kinds of content weakens your design and can confuse readers. To see what I mean, let's look at some of the key elements we commonly encounter.

PARAGRAPHS

Ah, the humble paragraph, the basic building block for most web pages. Paragraphs come in many shapes, sizes, and categories, but for now, let's talk about the kinds you commonly see for running text in articles.

Paragraphs are where we spend the most time when we read, so we need to be certain we're using a typeface that is comfortable for a long stay. This isn't too difficult a task; it's more a matter of not making something *uncomfortable* to read. Luckily, we have a lot of leeway: choosing a sturdy typeface and setting it well will get you there almost every time. Typefaces with less flourish and a uniform shape make for pleasing reading experiences, as they fade into the background and let the text take center stage.

As we saw in the last chapter, picking paragraph typefaces means looking closely at the letterforms in action. Less is usually more—we're not looking to impress anyone with our paragraph styles.

FIG 5.1 shows a fine start for paragraph styling. We have a good type size, a simple typeface choice of Chaparral, sufficient contrast with the background color, and decent spacing between the lines. Where we eventually end up with our paragraph style

I think that at that time none of us quite believed in the Time Machine. The fact is, the Time Traveller was one of those men who are too clever to be believed: you never felt that you saw all round him; you always suspected some subtle reserve, some ingenuity in ambush, behind his lucid frankness.

FIG 5.1: A simple, pleasing paragraph style set in Chaparral.

depends on other factors like intended use, device size, alignment, and more. We'll look at those considerations in Chapter 6.

Type size

So, what's a good font size? Is there a universal sweet spot, or is everything circumstantial? As we learned with the em box, numerical sizes can be deceiving since they don't always reflect what a typeface actually looks like.

The best way to approach sizing is to consider the reader and the reading distance. Most people sit about 18-24 inches away from their screens when it comes to a desktop; for mobile devices, it's a bit less (FIG 5.2). Put simply: the farther we are from our device, the larger the affordance of type size.

Considering the typical distance and common text sizes in printed matter—about 10 points or roughly 13 pixels, which reflects shorter reading distances—I tend to make my base type size 16 or 18 pixels, or 1-1.2 ems. I've listed fixed pixel units so we have a shared understanding of roughly how big the body text should be. In your own work, however, it's still best to use ems, *rems* (root em, whose value is relative to the html element), or percentages—all of whose relative sizes let you better respond to a gamut of devices and viewports. You can still use pixels when your elements require a specific size. Otherwise, relative units

FIG 5.2: The reading distance and type sizes from a desktop monitor are roughly comparable to those of a magazine held at arm's length. Photograph courtesy of Wilson Miner (http://bkaprt.com/owt/48/).

give the greatest control over keeping your sizing flexible while allowing users to resize text and pages within their browsers. For more on ems and rems, check out Jeremy Church's article on the topic (http://bkaprt.com/owt/49/).

In general, I would rather err on the side of making something too large than risk it being too small. When in doubt, make it bigger. This is true few times in design, but I've often found it to be the case in designing for the screen. Don't tell your clients though.

Measure and line-height

Conventional wisdom is to aim for a 45-75 character *measure* (the length of a line of text) on average in your running text, depending on the particular font, size, and setting. While you can go above or below that range—some news websites capably accommodate measures in the 80s—it's a good yardstick. That

I think that at that time none of us quite believed in the Time Machine. The fact is, the Time Traveller was one of those men who are too clever to be believed: you never felt that you saw all round him; you always suspected some subtle reserve, some ingenuity in ambush, behind his lucid frankness.

I think that at that time none of us quite believed in the Time Machine. The fact is, the Time Traveller was one of those men who are too clever to be believed...

FIG 5.3: A longer measure needs a bit more line spacing than a shorter one.

range exists because of the motion an eye makes from the end of one line to the start of the next. As lines contain more characters and grow longer, it's harder for a reader's eyes to successfully make the trip.

If you do need to use a longer measure, you'll want to balance it out by increasing the amount of space between lines (`line-height`). The extra spacing gives the reader's eyes room to make the trip and reduces the chance of losing their place along the way (**FIG 5.3**).

Similarly, if you're on the shorter end of the spectrum, you can get away with less `line-height`, since the distance from line end to line beginning is a shorter trip (**FIG 5.4**).

Awareness of `line-height` is especially important when dealing with responsive websites. As blocks of content expand and contract, you may need to adjust `line-height` values along with the `font-size` to ensure the type remains at a comfortable measure.

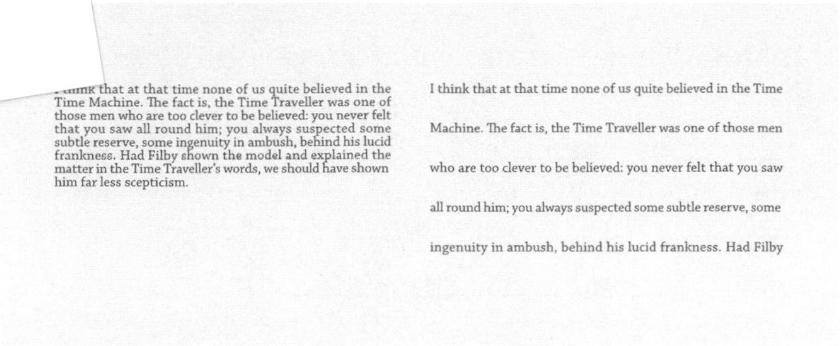

think that at that time none of us quite believed in the Time Machine. The fact is, the Time Traveller was one of those men who are too clever to be believed: you never felt that you saw all round him; you always suspected some subtle reserve, some ingenuity in ambush, behind his lucid frankness. Had Filby shown the model and explained the matter in the Time Traveller's words, we should have shown him far less scepticism.

I think that at that time none of us quite believed in the Time Machine. The fact is, the Time Traveller was one of those men who are too clever to be believed: you never felt that you saw all round him; you always suspected some subtle reserve, some ingenuity in ambush, behind his lucid frankness. Had Filby

FIG 5.4: Line spacing that's too tight makes text feel dense and congested, while line spacing that's too loose makes the lines feel like disconnected elements.

We'll touch on responsive design and the effects on measure and `line-height` in the next chapter.

A true ideal `line-height` doesn't exist, because every typeface is different. You need to take into account the design of the typeface as well as the typesetting. Is this a wide or decorative typeface? You may need more space between lines to let the details breathe. Is this a narrow text column, as you might see in hanging captions in an article's margins? You could use a smaller type size and keep the `line-height` tighter than the article text next to the caption. By observing these factors, you can judge what a particular setting requires.

A good starting point with `line-height` is about 1.2–1.8. It's best to omit units for `line-height`, as its values can get messy by dint of CSS's cascading properties (see CSS Tricks' Almanac for specifics (http://bkaprt.com/owt/50/). It takes some trial and error to see what's right for a given typeface at a given size in a given situation. I find it useful to declare a `line-height` and see how it feels to read text at that setting. Do letter ascenders and descenders crash into one another or run a little too close between lines? If so, more `line-height` is needed. Are the spaces between the lines more prominent than the lines themselves? If so, try reducing the `line-height`. When you find an appropriate `line-height`, the text will seem to fall into a natural rhythm, feeling neither too far apart nor too close.

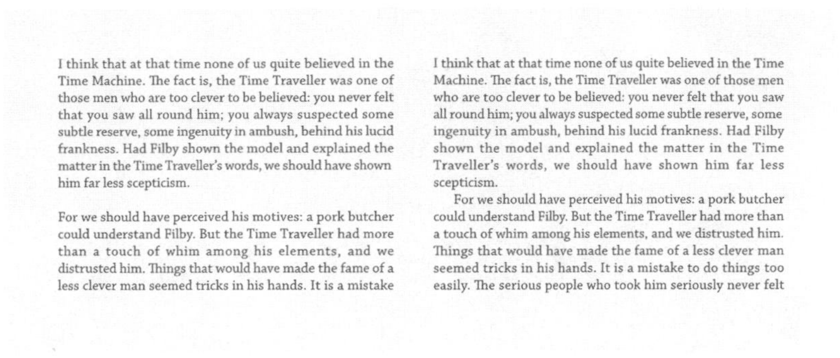

I think that at that time none of us quite believed in the Time Machine. The fact is, the Time Traveller was one of those men who are too clever to be believed: you never felt that you saw all round him; you always suspected some subtle reserve, some ingenuity in ambush, behind his lucid frankness. Had Filby shown the model and explained the matter in the Time Traveller's words, we should have shown him far less scepticism.

For we should have perceived his motives: a pork butcher could understand Filby. But the Time Traveller had more than a touch of whim among his elements, and we distrusted him. Things that would have made the fame of a less clever man seemed tricks in his hands. It is a mistake

I think that at that time none of us quite believed in the Time Machine. The fact is, the Time Traveller was one of those men who are too clever to be believed: you never felt that you saw all round him; you always suspected some subtle reserve, some ingenuity in ambush, behind his lucid frankness. Had Filby shown the model and explained the matter in the Time Traveller's words, we should have shown him far less scepticism.

For we should have perceived his motives: a pork butcher could understand Filby. But the Time Traveller had more than a touch of whim among his elements, and we distrusted him. Things that would have made the fame of a less clever man seemed tricks in his hands. It is a mistake to do things too easily. The serious people who took him seriously never felt

FIG 5.5: Two common ways to denote paragraphs: a blank line between paragraphs or an indent of the first line.

Indents and blank lines

There are several ways to denote a new paragraph, from outdented first lines to actual paragraph marks (¶), called *pilcrows*. On the web, these approaches skew toward either a blank line between paragraphs or an indent of the first line (**FIG 5.5**). While there is no right way to mark a new paragraph—it's largely based on personal preference or house style—it's a solid idea to reinforce common patterns, because people know what they mean.

Writing on the web tends to be more "chunked," where each paragraph holds a complete thought—as opposed to something like fiction, where a full line break may disrupt dialogue—so paragraphs can stand farther apart. As a bonus, these bite-sized chunks prove useful for skimming content.

If you use a blank line, make it equal to your type size or a touch smaller. For a first-line indent, it's customary to indent about 1 em. Again, this falls to personal preference. The crucial thing is making the distinction of the new paragraph apparent.

I like to think of paragraphs as akin to the underlying drumbeat in a song. They lay the groundwork for other kinds of content. Building outward, let's talk about a common paragraph companion: the headline.

Articles   Notes   Info   Search

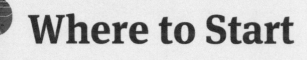

Where to Start

When making the transition to building responsive websites, the hardest part can be getting started.

I get my fair share of questions about how to choose a direction and chart out the first few steps from industry comrades and potential clients. It can seem daunting, so I thought I'd attempt to sum up a few of my own current thoughts on the matter.

FIG 5.6: Headlines on Trent Walton's website (http://bkaprt.com/owt/51/).

Headlines

Headlines are the attention grabbers. People skim them to decide whether or not to keep reading. Headlines come in a variety of forms, from straightforward article headings and subheadings to big marketing taglines and everything in between.

The headline marks the starting line for a text. It orients readers and serves as a kind of handshake and smile. It's your first chance to make an impression (**FIG 5.6**). A headline should not only distinguish itself from other text on the page (so as not to confuse the eye), but also help anchor the page as a whole. For the most part, headlines appear as larger text, but you can also opt to emphasize them through weight, spacing, alignment, or

Strange new paradox

The thing the Time Traveller held in his hand was a glittering metallic framework, scarcely larger than a small clock, and very delicately made. There was ivory in it, and some transparent crystalline substance.

Fourth dimensional voyage

And now I must be explicit, for this that follows—unless his explanation is to be accepted—is an absolutely unaccountable thing. He took one of the small octagonal tables that were scattered about the room, and set it in front of the fire, with two legs on the hearthrug. On this table he placed the mechanism. Then he drew up a chair, and sat down. The only other object on the table was a small shaded lamp, the bright light of which fell full upon

FIG 5.7: A headline at 32 pixels, subhead at 16 pixels, and text at 12 pixels.

---

color. A small headline can flatten your hierarchy and stunt one of your visual system's strongest tools. But a sturdy headline welcomes readers and guides them through the text.

A headline is typically set at some ratio larger than the body text. I usually work in simple math, doubling or tripling the body text size to find a potential headline size. So, I may try a body text size of 12 pixels and a headline size of 32 pixels. We can even split some of the difference to get a subhead size of 16 pixels. Take these numbers as rough starters; you always need to scrutinize how they look when typeset (**FIG 5.7**).

Once you have your base headline size, you can establish relationships *between* headings and subheadings. A reader should be able to distinguish, even at a glance, the role of one element from another. The visual prominence of an element may not always reflect its semantic value, but key elements will often have greater visual weight than other page content. Happily, many of the visual relationships on the web come prebuilt, thanks to semantic markup: h1, h2, and so on. Your visual styling should reinforce those roles, which often means moving from the highest semantic element (h1) downward. That gives the reader a pathway through your content. If you set your h2 the same size as your h1, a reader may rightly think they've started a new article rather than a subsection.

In the last example (**FIG 5.7**), you can see that the headline is at the top, followed by some text, a subhead, and then more text. The difference in heading sizing provides enough contrast to set up this relationship. A reader can assume that the largest text is important because it appears first in the reading flow, and because it's so big. Also, the paragraphs are related not only because they both fall under the headings, but also because they're the same size. This is a subtle visual exchange, one that we encounter enough in life as to be ingrained in us.

Contrasts like those are shorthand methods for creating visual hierarchy and building a typographic system in your designs, which in turn will imbue your work with variety and structure. They may seem simple, but don't mistake simple for obvious.

Once I understand the general relationships between elements, I look at how my typeface choices can support them. For instance, if I need a typeface for headlines, I like to find something that both looks good large, to let the details of the typeface shine, and holds up against fluctuating word lengths.

For a typical news site with numerous articles, you need to be able to deal with headlines of varying lengths, names that may require punctuation or accented characters, cited works set in italics, and more. Your typeface choice must handle these with grace. A slightly condensed face can work well in these situations, because you can fit more characters on each line and avoid awkward line breaks. For instance, FF Meta Serif is a somewhat narrow face, which accommodates a couple more characters per line than a wider serif like Georgia does (**FIG 5.8**).

Many folks, myself included, tend to use sans serifs for headlines. It comes down to simple geometry: most sans serifs can be packed in tighter than serifs because the letters take up less space. This allows for more characters per line and a larger type size. As you see in **FIG 5.9**, FF Meta takes up a little less room than its serif counterpart at the same type size. It's a small gain,

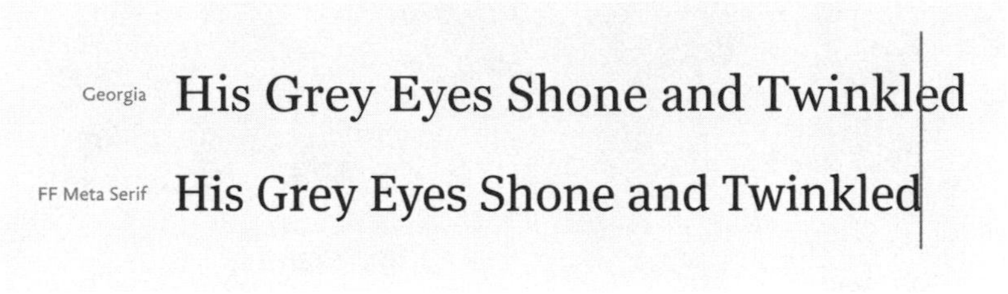

Georgia His Grey Eyes Shone and Twinkled

FF Meta Serif His Grey Eyes Shone and Twinkled

FIG 5.8: A narrower typeface like FF Meta Serif helps keep longer headlines from wrapping.

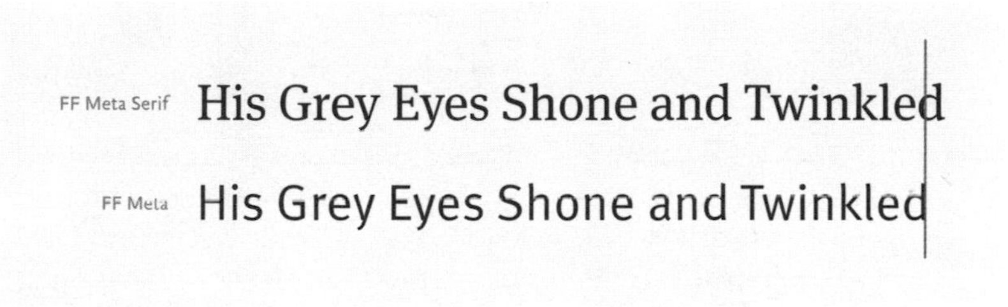

FF Meta Serif His Grey Eyes Shone and Twinkled

FF Meta His Grey Eyes Shone and Twinkled

FIG 5.9: Sans serif typefaces work well for headlines, because they often take up less horizontal space than serifs.

but it's enough to keep a word from wrapping to a new line and gives us a bit more space to make our headlines bigger.

Another kind of headline is more of an offshoot—it doesn't always accompany paragraphs and is sometimes quite large or decorative. It's a bit of an outlier and has more leeway to shake things up. I lump this into a category I like to call *big type.*

Big type

While big type is a kind of headline, it may not be atop an article. We often see these on homepages and splash pages for marketing sites.

Type this large is best considered in the same way you might a photograph: a picture of type that anchors a layout or creates the sort of mood you might spot on a movie poster or book cover.

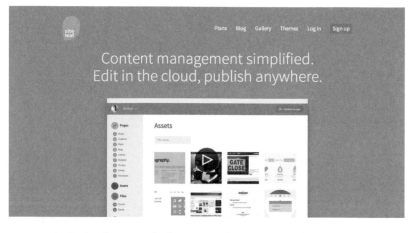

FIG 5.10: The big headline on Siteleaf's site is text that also acts as a large graphical element.

On Siteleaf (http://bkaprt.com/owt/52/), the headline is a large focal point for the page (**FIG 5.10**). It not only informs the reader, but also sets an open and welcoming atmosphere alongside the image. The big type complements the large screenshot through its proximity and color, creating a unified visual. Snappy headlines like these are the hallmarks of marketing design.

The same approaches for headlines apply here, with a couple of extra caveats. If you've been eyeing a decorative typeface, a one-off use here may be just the right amount of personality. Similarly, any errors in your text like incorrect punctuation (mind your smart quotes!) or bad line breaks will only be more apparent because they're larger. With responsive designs, it's also a good idea to tailor your line breaks. Visitors come to your site via all sorts of screen sizes, so consider customizing the type size and line breaks to keep the headline organized.

Go the extra mile and take care of how your headlines respond to varying screen sizes and conditions, rather than letting a browser handle the reflow. Some good ways to approach that level of detail are the jQuery plugins FitText and Lettering by Paravel or Font-to-Width by Nick Sherman and Chris Lewis.

FitText (http://bkaprt.com/owt/53/) allows an element's type size to increase or decrease in relation to its container so that it

FIG 5.11: FitText is a jQuery plugin that lets you size text up or down relative to its container.

completely fills the width. This additional control is especially handy when working responsively: your big, important headline is always full-width (**FIG 5.11**).

Font-to-Width (http://bkaprt.com/owt/54/) builds on similar concepts, but takes advantage of large type families by letting you specify a different typeface weight to fill a container's width instead of changing the type size. Both are useful in different situations: FitText changes your type's size, while Font-to-Width changes the actual font.

Lettering (http://bkaprt.com/owt/55/) wraps the individual letters of a specified element so that you can access them with CSS, allowing for some quick adjustments to kerning (the space

A jQuery plugin for radical web typography   DOWNLOAD ON GITHUB

FIG 5.12: Lettering is a jQuery plugin that appends dynamic classes to a given piece of text; you can style the classes individually with CSS.

between individual letters), colors of particular letters, or anything else you think up (**FIG 5.12**). Unlike in desktop applications for print design, we don't have much built-in control over kerning in CSS, as those settings mostly reside with the type designer. For limited use like a big headline, it's helpful to have more control over the way letters lock up, especially in difficult letter pairings that typically end up with extra space (e.g., most anything involving a capital *A* or *T*).

Obviously, you wouldn't want to use any of these plugins for a large amount of text. But for a crucial homepage headline, these methods give you the flexibility of a prepared image while retaining all the advantages of live text (as we saw in Chapter 2).

Some great new CSS values are also rolling out in browsers to support viewports, like vw (1vw = 1% of viewport width) and vh (1vh = 1% of viewport height), which let you achieve similar results without the need for JavaScript. Browser support for these values is still scarce, but it's on the rise. For more on this, check out Chris Coyier's article "Viewport Sized Typography" (http://bkaprt.com/owt/56/).

SMALL TYPE

Small type is comprised of an unassuming variety of supporting elements. Interface, which we'll cover shortly, is a common kind of small type, but article-specific categories like captions, footnotes, and asides are also important to distinguish.

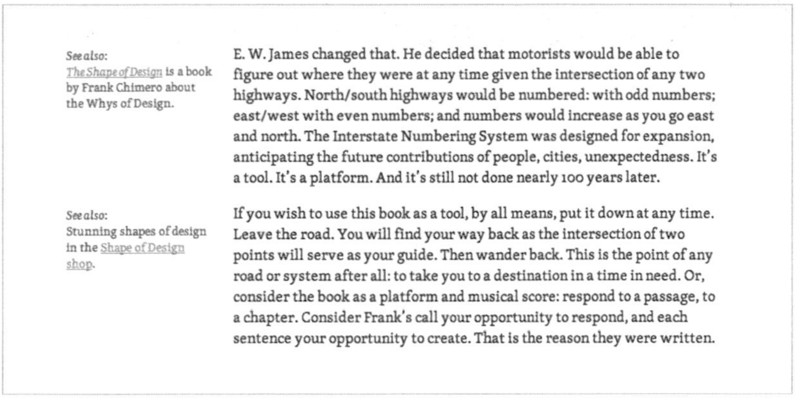

See also:
The Shape of Design is a book by Frank Chimero about the Whys of Design.

E. W. James changed that. He decided that motorists would be able to figure out where they were at any time given the intersection of any two highways. North/south highways would be numbered: with odd numbers; east/west with even numbers; and numbers would increase as you go east and north. The Interstate Numbering System was designed for expansion, anticipating the future contributions of people, cities, unexpectedness. It's a tool. It's a platform. And it's still not done nearly 100 years later.

See also:
Stunning shapes of design in the Shape of Design shop.

If you wish to use this book as a tool, by all means, put it down at any time. Leave the road. You will find your way back as the intersection of two points will serve as your guide. Then wander back. This is the point of any road or system after all: to take you to a destination in a time in need. Or, consider the book as a platform and musical score: respond to a passage, to a chapter. Consider Frank's call your opportunity to respond, and each sentence your opportunity to create. That is the reason they were written.

FIG 5.13: A simple caption treatment on Liz Danzico's site, Bobulate (http://bkaprt.com/owt/57/).

First, realize that small type serves a specific purpose. It marks a visual contrast and shift in tone—a separate point of information from a text's main stream. The change in size is equivalent to a change in the tone or volume of your voice when speaking. You're still the speaker, but this is something worth saying differently. A change in type size (which may be as simple as 80% of our base type size) signals that shift (**FIG 5.13**).

As this type is smaller, you need to be extra aware of your typeface choice. Test your type in context to make sure it remains legible and clean under your sizing conditions. You can use the same typeface as your body text if it holds up well to the smaller sizing, or choose something better suited to small sizes. Picking a separate caption typeface gives you the added ability to visually signal a change in voice—as when a side note comes from an editor instead of the author.

Another example of small type is the line of contact information, which can be important even if infrequently accessed (**FIG 5.14**). It doesn't need much prominence and, luckily, it's an accepted convention that contact information appears at the bottom of a page, so people know where to find it. As a result, the type can be small and understated if that serves your design.

FIG 5.14: A typical contact line.

One last note on small type: if we're talking about more than a few lines, small type may not be the way to go. Prolonged reading of small text gets cumbersome really fast. For quick asides and captions, though, it's perfect.

OTHER NOTABLE TYPES

For the rest of the common elements you may encounter, you can mix and match the approaches we've already looked at. Elements like `blockquote`, code, status messages in modal windows, and anything else outside the norm pop up from time to time. The biggest thing to remember with any other element is to evaluate its purpose, its importance, and where it appears in context.

In the case of a `blockquote`, some small-text principles apply (though it's less about size). A `blockquote` is a bit of text quoted outside of an article's main text. It's common to set a `blockquote` apart visually from the normal text to mark this change in voice, and this can be a good opportunity to switch from a serif to a sans serif (or vice versa, depending on your body typeface). In print, quotes are typically distinguished with indented text and italics, but on the web, the patterns can be more stylized. You can mark quotes with italics, a change in type size, a change in typeface, the addition of larger open and close quotation marks, a change in color or border, or any combination of the above.

In the case of pull quotes, you may even take an ornamental approach by setting the `blockquote` larger to add interest. These can be particularly effective in running text to add some variety to type and imagery (**FIG 5.15**). Pull quotes serve as a nice visual anchor and draw readers into the article.

Some of these styles are fine for a quote here or there, but if you're doing lots of quoting, a more subtle style (as we often see

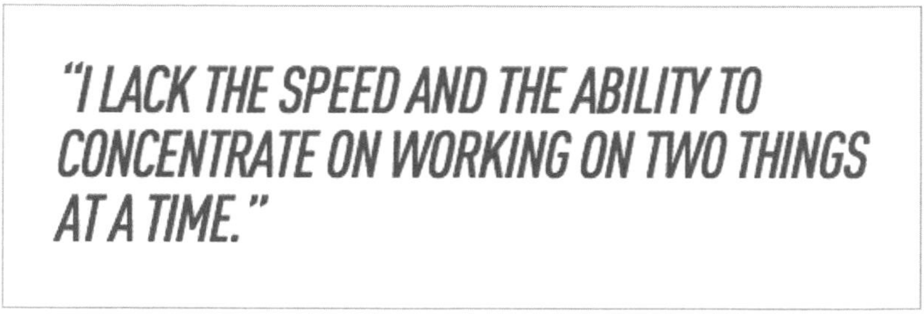

> # "I LACK THE SPEED AND THE ABILITY TO CONCENTRATE ON WORKING ON TWO THINGS AT A TIME."

FIG 5.15: A stylistic pull quote treatment grabs a skimming reader's attention (http://bkaprt.com/owt/58/).

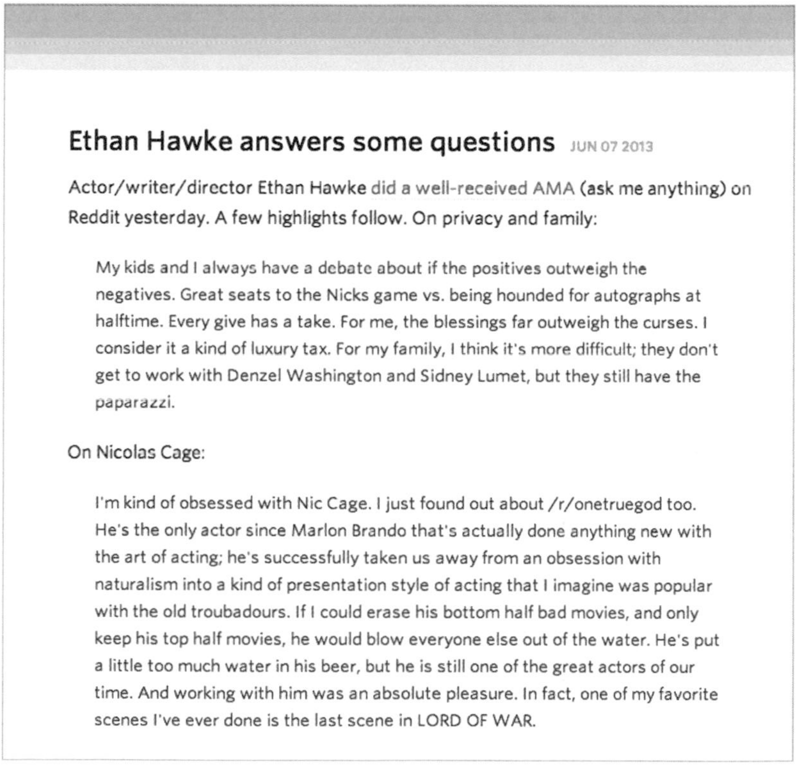

Ethan Hawke answers some questions JUN 07 2013

Actor/writer/director Ethan Hawke did a well-received AMA (ask me anything) on Reddit yesterday. A few highlights follow. On privacy and family:

> My kids and I always have a debate about if the positives outweigh the negatives. Great seats to the Nicks game vs. being hounded for autographs at halftime. Every give has a take. For me, the blessings far outweigh the curses. I consider it a kind of luxury tax. For my family, I think it's more difficult; they don't get to work with Denzel Washington and Sidney Lumet, but they still have the paparazzi.

On Nicolas Cage:

> I'm kind of obsessed with Nic Cage. I just found out about /r/onetruegod too. He's the only actor since Marlon Brando that's actually done anything new with the art of acting; he's successfully taken us away from an obsession with naturalism into a kind of presentation style of acting that I imagine was popular with the old troubadours. If I could erase his bottom half bad movies, and only keep his top half movies, he would blow everyone else out of the water. He's put a little too much water in his beer, but he is still one of the great actors of our time. And working with him was an absolute pleasure. In fact, one of my favorite scenes I've ever done is the last scene in LORD OF WAR.

FIG 5.16: A simple blockquote style on kottke.org (http://bkaprt.com/owt/59/).

in print) is probably a better choice to keep the article text and the quotes from fighting each other.

On Jason Kottke's website (**FIG 5.16**), you see probably the most common `blockquote` style, which makes the type a little smaller than the base type and lighter in color. This works well, because it's a simple visual change that marks a shift in voice while still feeling tied to the rest of the text.

So now we've got multiple ways to handle text-heavy content. But that's only one facet of the web. What about the elements that we not only read, but also click, tap, and otherwise interact with? That's right, cue interfaces!

INTERFACE

User interface (UI) refers to elements that enable actions and give context within a website or app (**FIG 5.17**). Common UI components include site navigation, buttons, form elements and labels, status messages, account links, and anything in between.

These elements serve a dual purpose: like paragraphs, they're content, but like headlines, they may be set large to nab attention or anchor a layout. For instance, the text in a button may be bigger or smaller than our base text size, depending on its purpose and place on the page. A button that supports a headline or call to action requires a more prominent visual style, whereas a button for compulsory secondary actions (log out, search, etc.) may figure smaller (**FIG 5.18**).

Because websites have various layers of UI elements depending on their function, we must gauge the visual weight needed to convey an element's idea and the hierarchy required for its purpose. Important UI elements like navigation may need more visual prominence than less frequently accessed elements like a logout button. That isn't to say they aren't both important, but we can visually rank these elements based on their use.

Even with a variety of uses and kinds, some conventions for these items do emerge. Many web apps tend to make UI text smaller so they can squeeze a lot of elements into a limited space. Keep the text legible above all else. What use is an important button if I can't read it?

FIG 5.17: Twitter's header shows common interface elements like a navigation bar and a search form.

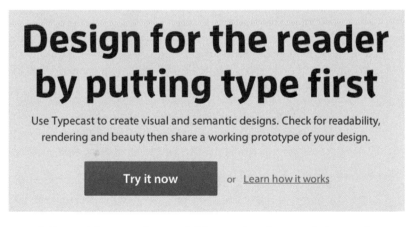

FIG 5.18: Typecast's homepage features a bright, prominent button and a less prominent secondary link in gray text (http://bkaprt.com/owt/60/).

Because of how quickly a header can become crowded with options (especially after signing into a site where more options are revealed), I favor sans serif typefaces for UI. As we saw earlier, they can be set smaller and a little tighter than serifs. And in these situations, every bit of space counts, especially if you need to translate your navigation labels into other languages.

There's no accepted size or styling for UI, because it depends on its purpose and importance. But no matter what kind of interface element we're talking about, we need to make it legible and recognizable to a user.

PUTTING IT ALL TOGETHER

Once you have your building blocks accounted for, you can assemble your typographic system and then focus on hierarchical relationships. Which elements are most important? What relationships do elements share? To figure this out, you can look at the markup and see what the semantic structure looks like. An h1 is likely our biggest and most important text, and then down the line to h2, h3, and so on.

That's fine for text, but what about navigational elements, images, and other kinds of content that need to fit in? Always think about your intent—the things you want a visitor to do—and use that to influence your visual styling.

If you want someone to read an article, focus your efforts on styling the text. Make sure it's nice and readable, with a clear entry point—like a big, appealing headline that shepherds readers into the article.

If you want someone to watch a video or register for an account, focus on making those elements shine. They don't need to be the biggest items on the page, but they should have enough heft and visual prominence through placement and color to draw attention.

Let's look at a content-heavy website like the *New York Times* and examine some of the decisions that give the design structure and flow (FIG 5.19).

Right off the bat, we see a few different kinds of content: past the masthead and navigation, we have a big headline and excerpt at the top left, some text with an accompanying large image in

FIG 5.19: The *New York Times'* homepage, a great example of hierarchy and contrast.

the middle, and some smaller articles listed on the top right. Using what we learned in the last chapter, you can pick up on the ways the site distinguishes various elements:

- On the top left, the large headline—set in italics for further distinction—quickly grabs a reader's attention and provides an entry point.
- Because of contrast, it's even more likely that a reader's eye is drawn to the middle image; its size and placement set it apart.
- Other text may be big, too, like secondary headlines, but that central, lone image is the page's focal point.

So, if mammoth type or images are surefire ways to pull in a reader, why don't we stuff our pages with them? If you think about it, that type and image are so alluring *because* they're unique. If we bombarded the page with more images and an army of big headlines, each would bear the same weight and cancel out any contrast. Without contrast, we don't have hierarchy, and without hierarchy, the typography feels indistinguishable and our readers are left without a map.

On the *New York Times* site, contrasts in type size, style, and placement apply structure to its content and set up relationships. When we first glance at something, we tend to seek patterns; we mentally group similar elements and try to uncover a pecking order.

Titles on the *New York Times* homepage are set large, with key headlines closer to the top. Subheadings and bylines tie into the headline at smaller sizes but remain visually distinct from paragraphs. This styling underscores that the subheading is part of the same system as the headline, while establishing that the subheading is hierarchically less important. The paragraph excerpts tap into this same hierarchical system; while their type size is even smaller than that of the subheading, the paragraphs are set and styled the same as one another. This consistency means readers quickly understand that these chunks are similar kinds of content.

I've noted simple arrangements here, but, together, they form the backbone of a strong typographic system built on relationships. All of typography is based upon a reflexive relationship: the small things inform the big things, and the big things inform the small things. The sum of this give and take means the difference between beautiful and forgettable.

We've covered the most important typographic considerations you can make at the micro level. But what about the other end of the spectrum: *the page?* How do larger elements, like the browser window or grid systems, affect our lovingly crafted paragraphs and headlines? Let's look at the big picture.

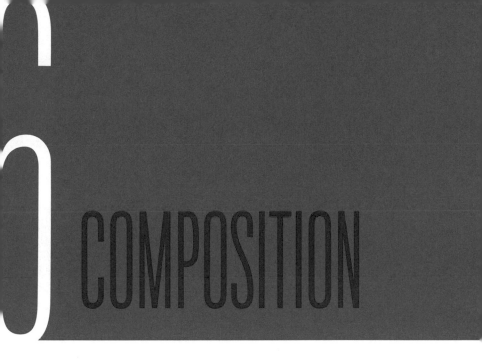

COMPOSITION

TYPE HELPS form the message our designs seek to impart, but it resides in a larger environment made up of a page, a browser, and a device. From the outside looking in, we understand that our text, our fonts, and our beautiful typography do not exist in a vacuum. The shape of our design and the web's fluctuating nature directly influence our typographic choices and everything we hope we convey.

Depending on the problems we're trying to solve, our approach can take different forms. Sometimes our process follows a straightforward and ordered path, especially given the number of fixed constraints a project may impose, like ad sizes or required artwork and assets. Other times, our process is more malleable, like working with clay. A sculptor may sit down to sculpt something without a clear idea of the exact form it will take; sometimes we need to start pushing and pulling on the clay to see what comes out of it.

I often work in what I consider rough typographic explorations, even if they're in a high-fidelity environment like

Photoshop or a browser, to see how the content speaks to me and if it becomes apparent how it wants to be set. Just as planks of wood have a grain to observe when you're building something, so too does our content.

Whatever path we embark on, composition of our layout and typographic systems needs to take our medium's constraints into account.

KNOWN UNKNOWNS

If we all sat down and read the same printed book, we'd likely experience it under similar constraints. We'd be limited to the same page size, type, and layout. Printed books are a static format. From the designer's initial layout of the book to its trip to the press bed, the warehouse, the bookshelf, and your hands, the output of that book doesn't change. It's delivered exactly as the designer conceived it. That's consistency you can plan around, and it builds on principles of mass production that have held constant for many decades.

Compare that with any website. If we were all to visit the same site, what we each see would be determined by a number of cascading factors, like our chosen device (desktop, mobile, tablet, etc.), the physical screen size, the screen resolution, our chosen browser, the size of the browser window, the browser settings, and more. Some of these factors can cause drastic differences in our experiences. Some may give us the impression that the type is too small, others may cause us to miss something important just off screen, and still others may make it nearly impossible to view the web page at all.

These factors are at once a blessing and a curse. For those of us making websites, they can cause seemingly endless, frustrating hours of debugging code, and for those of us viewing, they can stand in the way of doing something as simple as reading the news.

But, understanding that these things are baked into the way the web works gives us tremendous power. We can tailor our content to adapt to virtually any screen size and to look pretty good while doing so. Sure, it's more difficult to achieve the set precision you get with designing for a physical book's single size, but we gain the advantage of having a design that can potentially be viewed by almost anyone, anywhere, on anything. All of these factors prove to be a challenge for managing typography. How can you ensure that your type feels right on any screen?

RESPONSIVE TYPOGRAPHY

While the full gamut of responsive design falls outside of this book's scope, it's important to briefly go over its effects on typography, namely: sizing. Though I'm framing this around the idea of responsive design, the same principles apply to stand-alone mobile sites, applications, and any specialized version of your website targeted at various devices. This includes your site's design at its largest size on a huge screen, the myriad in-between breakpoints, all the way down to the smallest, palm-sized screen.

As your site responds to various displays and devices, your type needs to maintain its integrity and adapt with the layout. As we saw in Chapter 5, you can relieve many sizing headaches by using relative units like ems or percentages for type, the widths of columns, and the widths of other page elements. This keeps your hierarchy intact as your designs and typography grow and shrink in size. It's still a catch-all method though, so you may need to tailor your sizing to ensure a better experience and visual lockup.

Happily, you have help—and you can still rely on some constants. With the advent of responsive web design, you can use CSS media queries to specify breakpoints and tailor your container widths—and thus the widths of the lines of text inside those containers—to always be an appropriate length. The 45-75 characters per line range is still a good starting point, but you'll need to see what that looks like in a typeface at a given size. If your line lengths grow longer at larger breakpoints, your type size should increase too. Conversely, as your line lengths shorten, your type size can decrease.

You may, however, need to further adjust your `line-height` to suit unknown screens. The `line-height` that worked so well at a display size for your desktop may appear too large on a smaller

FIG 6.1: The type size and line lengths in Trent Walton's design subtly adapt depending on the screen or device size (http://bkaprt.com/owt/61/).

phone display. You might need to compensate to make things look right. If you're sticking with a typical `line-height` of 1.5, you might nudge it down to 1.2 or 1.3 on smaller screens, as you'll have shorter line lengths that won't need as much breathing room.

On designer Trent Walton's site, his base type size gets quite large on a big monitor, 137.5% with a 1.6 `line-height`, but as the page or device width gets smaller, the base font size drops to 100% with a 1.4 `line-height` to better accommodate the shorter line lengths (**FIG 6.1**).

Methods like these are simple to implement but powerful, because they can govern so much of your typography's visual presentation. Type and all of your page elements can be spun out of these relative measurements. That links everything together like *Powers of Ten,* as the small influences the big and the big influences the small. So whenever the screen, device, or parameters change, your design responds. And whenever you need to make changes, you can alter the way your layout works by modifying only a few values.

No matter which device someone is viewing your work on, you want to give them the best experience possible. Luckily, type is like water flowing into a glass; it fills whatever container you put it in. You just have to make sure the content suits the width of the container. But how do several containers on the same page affect your typography?

COMPOSING THE PAGE

Understanding the constraints in our medium informs our design approach and better prepares us for things we can't plan for. One of the best ways to help our design system serve as a solid foundation is to equip ourselves with a layout plan. That's right, everyone's favorite design topic: grids!

Grids for layout

Much has been written about the use of grids, and rightly so. They're handy as all get-out and also one of the most misunderstood design elements. A grid helps you organize your content and reinforce your typographic hierarchy. While hierarchy lets you plan your typography at a micro level, a grid allows you to arrange the type and everything else it interacts with on the page at a macro level. It helps readers traverse content and exposes an informational system to them. For example, if you use a grid and your headlines always appear in a certain spot or your images always appear at certain dimensions, readers can recognize that consistency. Those patterns are signposts that light the way for viewers to find what they're looking for in the content and to distinguish between elements.

Grids have gotten a bad rap because, on the surface, they appear too restrictive a tool for layout. Many folks are still under the impression that grids limit and force a designer to simply fill out prearranged buckets with content and images, like a design paint-by-number kit. To the uninitiated, that may be the case; a grid looks like little more than a rigid framework. But a grid's power lies in the suggestion of flow and alignment. A grid does not dictate where elements go; it merely serves as a collection of possibilities (FIG 6.2).

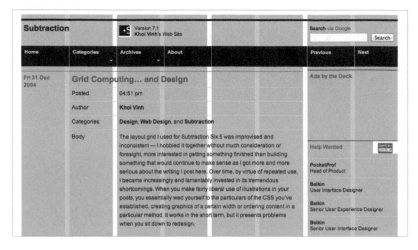

FIG 6.2: Khoi Vinh's Subtraction uses a basic eight-column grid (http://bkaprt.com/owt/62/).

A grid allows you to frame your layout with purpose to align page elements and build hierarchical relationships. Put plainly, a grid is an essential building block for intentional design.

Many kinds of grid systems exist, though you may be most familiar with a *column grid*. Most grid frameworks for the web consist of uniform vertical columns spaced evenly across a page. But as you can see in **FIG 6.3**, this is only one type. *Modular grids* are similar to column grids but have lots of horizontal lines that divide columns into a matrix of modules. *Hierarchical grids* organize disparate kinds of flexible content (cue dramatic music: like a web page!) based on their needs to grow and shrink, rather than at regular intervals.

I often use a combination of grids in my work. For instance, on my personal site, I employ a hierarchical grid to layer elements like a cake, and within that, I sometimes use a column grid to vertically organize things.

A hierarchical grid slats horizontal modules vertically one after another, moving down the page. This linear procession, like Hansel and Gretel leaving a trail of bread crumbs, gently leads a viewer down a path. The vertical flow from top to bottom

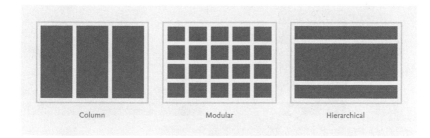

| Column | Modular | Hierarchical |

FIG 6.3: Some common kinds of grid systems for the web.

FIG 6.4: My site with a hierarchical grid overlay (left), and a column grid overlay (right).

FIG 6.5: A grid system lets you improvise on a consistent structure to achieve varied layouts.

The Grid System					
The ultimate resource in grid systems.		"The grid system is an aid, not a guarantee. It permits a number of possible uses and each designer can look for a solution appropriate to his personal style. But one must learn how to use the grid; it is an art that requires practice." Josef Müller-Brockmann		POWERING THE QUALITY WEB WITH BEAUTIFUL ADS. Reach the best creative audience around. Try InfluAds. Powered by InfluAds	
Articles	Tools	Books	Templates	Blog	Inspiration
The 960 Grid System Made Easy	Golden Grid System	An Initiation in Typography	Photoshop Grid Templates	New RSS Feed	Ace Jet 170
This article is for web designers and front-end web developers who are interested in grid-based layout systems but are at a loss on how to decipher them. 04.Mar.2012	A folding grid for responsive design. 04.Mar.2012	In this fascinating initiation into visual design and typography. The first chapter deals with proportions: grid systems and typographical measurements. 04.Mar.2012	A small collection of grid templates for various devices and common design scenarios. 04.Mar.2012	Hi folks, the RSS Feed has been migrated to new service. If you are subscribed to the old Feedburner URL, please unsubscribe and subscribe to the new URL: thegridsystem.org/feed/. 05.Sep.2013	AisleOne / Athletics / BBDK / Blanka / Build / Corporate Risk Watch / Counter Print / David Airey / Design Assembly / Dirty Mouse / Experimental Jetset / Form Fifty Five
How You Make A Grid	Fluid Baseline Grid System	Ordering Disorder: Grid Principles for Web Design	960px Grid Templates	Khoi Vinh — On the grid	Grafik Magazine
A PDF written by Andrew Maher to help you design grids and to give you the resources to delve further into the grid world. 04.Mar.2012	An HTML5 & CSS3 development kit that provides a solid foundation to quickly design websites with ease. 04.Mar.2012	Ordering Disorder is a book by Khoi Vinh that delivers a definitive take on grids and the Web and provides both the big ideas and techniques of grid-based design. 11.Nov.2010	A selection of 960 pixel-wide uniform grid templates ranging from 3-columns to 16-columns, for both Adobe Photoshop and Fireworks. 11.Nov.2010	Web and interactive designer Khoi Vinh speaks about his process and using the grid. 04.Mar.2012	Grain Edit / Graphic Hug / I Love Typography / Lamosca / Mark Boulton / Minimal Sites / Monocle / Neubau / NewWork / OK-RM

FIG 6.6: The Grid System site uses a basic six-column grid with an underlying baseline grid (http://bkaprt.com/owt/63/).

focuses the design on one message—in this case, the article—and reinforces a natural hierarchy. As a bonus, a hierarchical grid easily lends itself to the stacked, one-column layouts common in responsive web design's smaller breakpoints (**FIG 6.4**). But a page is multidimensional, and we must also consider the horizontal axis. For my site, I used a column grid in addition to the hierarchical grid to organize elements across the page. For instance, the columns provide regular intervals to space elements out, but also separate different content types like columns of body text or sidebars. These divisions are especially effective for the large footer and complex articles, because they extend the design system to have more possibilities inside the hierarchical grid's layer cake (**FIG 6.5**).

That's a quick tour of grids, but their usefulness cannot be understated. If a design is to provide a clear message, its form must be clear as well. A layout grid helps us put our best face forward. I have one last grid I want to touch on, and it's a special one just for type.

Baseline grids

A *baseline grid* is a series of rows spun out of the spacing between baselines in text, or the invisible line that letters sit on. It's a means to horizontally align all the type on the page, including captions, headlines, and running text (**FIG 6.6**).

In print, baseline grids evolved to serve two purposes: to provide a consistent rhythm to text as it cascades down a page, and, more important, to deal with the printed page's inherent translucency. As light shines through a printed page, text aligned on the same grid on both sides of the paper keeps the text from looking distorted. If the text were misaligned, you'd see the faint whisper of reversed text through the page.

But do these constraints apply to a web page?

The first point on vertical rhythm is debatable, at least when it comes to web design. The more variables you throw at a baseline grid, the harder it is to use. A single typeface at various sizes aligns to the grid easily enough. But once you add a second typeface, you have to contend with the properties specific to each of them. One typeface may require more spacing than the other, which may not work with your baseline grid. Add images, videos, and other assets of varying dimensions to a page, and the difficulty in maintaining the baseline grid compounds. The second point about page translucency and ghostly text is moot on a screen.

Further, layout applications typically used for print, like Adobe InDesign, boast many more affordances to automate using a baseline grid. A designer can easily establish styles to break out of the grid as needed, and get back on rhythm afterward—as you might see in a large headline that goes off-grid and breaks to multiple lines. On the web, CSS isn't optimized to achieve this level of control yet, and any attempts to emulate it usually lead to a mire of additional rules and headaches.

So, when should you use baseline grids on the web? Perhaps the best use case is aligning columns of text that appear next to each other, as with multicolumn websites or secondary elements (e.g., pull quotes and sidebars). The baseline grid keeps a consistent rhythm vertically across the horizontal blocks. Overall, however, I've found baseline grids more trouble than they're worth.

Unlike the physical page, the web is a fluid medium, and baseline grids seek to reinforce an idealized web where the designer has ultimate control over the reading experience. Factors like browser rendering, layout interpretations, image sizes, ad sizes, and general unforeseen wonkiness make employing a baseline grid pretty time intensive. You can achieve rhythm through size and spacing just as well. The most important thing to shoot for, whether you use a baseline grid or not, is a nice even texture and pacing to your design.

ALIGNMENT AND HYPHENATION

Now that we've looked at how to pace content with various grids, we must also examine how type responds to its container's width when line breaks occur and the various options for text alignment. Currently, we have four basic alignment types: `left`, `right`, `centered`, and `justify` (**FIG 6.7**). *Left, right,* and *centered* refer to where the text aligns, and these styles include uneven "ragged"

He took one of the small octagonal tables that were scattered about the room, and set it in front of the fire, with two legs on the hearthrug. On this table he placed the mechanism. Then he drew up a chair, and sat down. The only other object on the table was a small shaded lamp, the bright light of which fell full

Flush left, ragged right

He took one of the small octagonal tables that were scattered about the room, and set it in front of the fire, with two legs on the hearthrug. On this table he placed the mechanism. Then he drew up a chair, and sat down. The only other object on the table was a small shaded lamp, the bright light of which

Flush right, ragged left

He took one of the small octagonal tables that were scattered about the room, and set it in front of the fire, with two legs on the hearthrug. On this table he placed the mechanism. Then he drew up a chair, and sat down. The only other object on the table was a small shaded lamp, the bright light of which

Centered

He took one of the small octagonal tables that were scattered about the room, and set it in front of the fire, with two legs on the hearthrug. On this table he placed the mechanism. Then he drew up a chair, and sat down. The only other object on the table was a small shaded lamp, the bright light of which fell full

Justified

FIG 6.7: Types of text alignment.

edges. *Justified text* aligns to both the left and right sides of its container by expanding or compressing the spaces on each line.

Most magazine and book text is justified and makes ample use of hyphenation, as it creates pleasing shapes from the text blocks and is an efficient use of space. Until recently, this has been very difficult to do on the web. Hyphenation wasn't readily available, and—depending on factors like font selection and size—justification could produce less desirable results (**FIG 6.8**).

Things have progressed a little, and you can now enable crude hyphenation with CSS:

```
-webkit-hyphens: auto;
-moz-hyphens: auto;
hyphens: auto;
```

Be forewarned: the results are unpredictable. Desktop applications like InDesign have extensive libraries and options that let you configure hyphenation thresholds to avoid undesirable results, like multiple sequential lines that end in hyphens. But on the web, we don't have anything that approaches that flexibility yet. So while at first blush a hyphenated text block may seem to

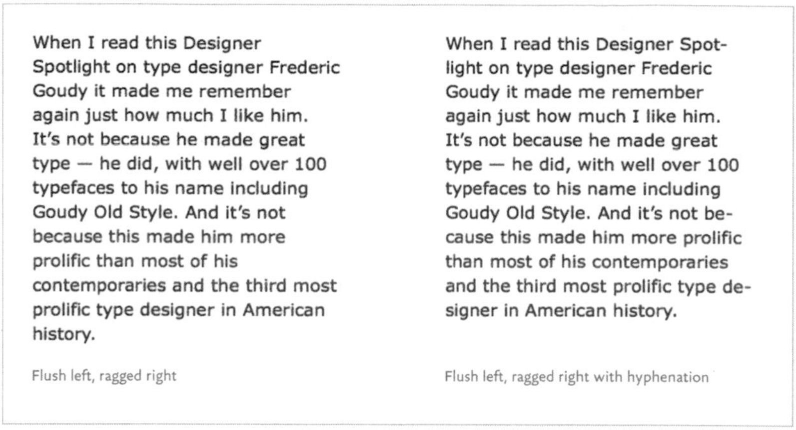

When I read this Designer
Spotlight on type designer Frederic
Goudy it made me remember
again just how much I like him.
It's not because he made great
type — he did, with well over 100
typefaces to his name including
Goudy Old Style. And it's not
because this made him more
prolific than most of his
contemporaries and the third most
prolific type designer in American
history.

Flush left, ragged right

When I read this Designer Spotlight on type designer Frederic
Goudy it made me remember
again just how much I like him.
It's not because he made great
type — he did, with well over 100
typefaces to his name including
Goudy Old Style. And it's not because this made him more prolific
than most of his contemporaries
and the third most prolific type designer in American history.

Flush left, ragged right with hyphenation

FIG 6.8: CSS hyphenation is a balancing act. Hyphenation may create more pleasing shapes
for text, but it may also break words in unexpected places (http://bkaprt.com/owt/64/).

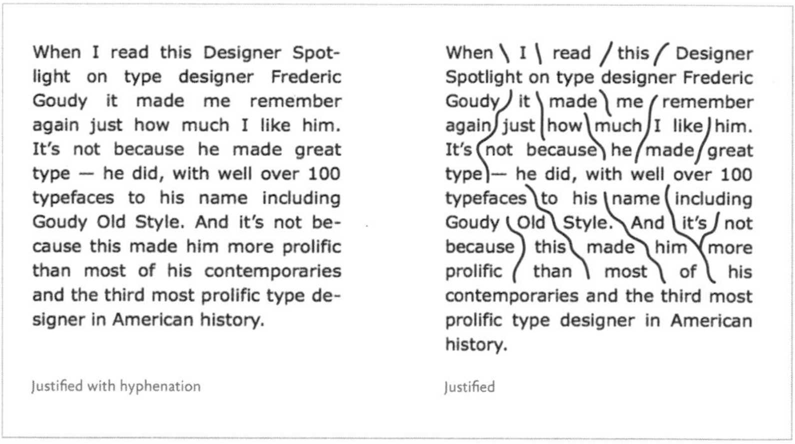

When I read this Designer Spotlight on type designer Frederic
Goudy it made me remember
again just how much I like him.
It's not because he made great
type — he did, with well over 100
typefaces to his name including
Goudy Old Style. And it's not because this made him more prolific
than most of his contemporaries
and the third most prolific type designer in American history.

Justified with hyphenation

When \ I \ read / this / Designer
Spotlight on type designer Frederic
Goudy / it \ made \ me / remember
again / just | how \ much / I like / him.
It's (not because\ he / made / great
type)— he did, with well over 100
typefaces \ to his | name (including
Goudy (Old \ Style. \ And \ it's / not
because) this \ made \ him \ more
prolific (than \ most \ of \ his
contemporaries and the third most
prolific type designer in American
history.

Justified

FIG 6.9: By default, justified text on the web doesn't provide the fine control you may see
with a desktop publishing application, yielding unsightly rivers in your paragraphs (right).

create a more pleasing shape on the page, once you settle in to read, you may find some awkward line breaks.

Justification suffers from a similar lack of fine control. In a world of publishing that still relies on templates to make sense of dynamic text dumped out of a CMS, we do little more than cross our fingers for a good result when justifying text.

Beyond CSS, many scripts out there can programmatically do a better job hyphenating text, but you'll need to weigh the addition of another page asset against nicer line breaks.

The narrower the text column, the more the problems with justification and hyphenation are exacerbated. Varying word lengths, unpredictable reading environments, custom settings, and unknown font substitutions can produce an unexpected collection of *rivers,* or apparent openings cascading vertically through text (**FIG 6.9**).

Both justified type and hyphenation are very potent tools in laying out type, but be sure they work well with the typefaces you use and their settings in your design.

TYPOGRAPHIC COLOR

Every typeface has *color,* and when set, it gives the overall page a color too. I'm not referring to an actual hue; I mean the *gray value.* To see what it looks like, squint your eyes at the bits of text in **FIG 6.10**.

I've provided a little cheat sheet in the form of the gray circle above each text block. That gray value is the text's typographic color. Color is created by both the letterforms themselves (some fonts may have more color if their letterforms have heavy strokes, high contrast between thicks and thins, or a larger x-height) and their settings (tight lines or letter-spacing may make a passage feel darker).

You don't want to overwhelm a design, call too much attention to the type, or create running text that is too high in contrast, so I find it's best to strive for a medium gray value.

Fonts with less color may need a tighter `line-height` to carry more weight, and fonts with more color can usually do with a bit more `line-height` to temper their heaviness (**FIG 6.11**).

The best text faces have some personality but not so much that they distract us from the content or the reading experience. Typefaces with a lot of personality are better reserved for display sizes, as they can be cumbersome to read in longer passages. The usual

The best text faces have some personality but not so much that they distract us from the content or the reading experience. Typefaces with a lot of personality are better reserved for display sizes, as they can be cumbersome to read in longer passages. The usual conventions for selecting type apply to screen use too, but due to the disparity in quality

The best text faces have some personality but not so much that they distract us from the content or the reading experience. Typefaces with a lot of personality are better reserved for display sizes, as they can be cumbersome to read in longer passages. The usual conventions for selecting type apply to screen use too, but due to the disparity in quality between the screen and a printed page, those conventions should be followed even more closely and possibly a little exaggerated. High x-height and a strong character body

FIG 6.10: Typefaces have inherent typographic color values that come from their shapes and typesetting.

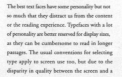

The best text faces have some personality but not so much that they distract us from the content or the reading experience. Typefaces with a lot of personality are better reserved for display sizes, as they can be cumbersome to read in longer passages. The usual conventions for selecting type apply to screen use too, but due to the disparity in quality between the screen and a

Adobe Garamond

The best text faces have some personality but not so much that they distract us from the content or the reading experience. Typefaces with a lot of personality are better reserved for display sizes, as they can be cumbersome to read in longer passages. The usual conventions for selecting type apply to screen use too, but due to the disparity in

Myriad Pro

The best text faces have some personality but not so much that they distract us from the content or the reading experience. Typefaces with a lot of personality are better reserved for display sizes, as they can be cumbersome to read in longer passages. The usual conventions for selecting type apply to screen use too,

Helvetica Neue

FIG 6.11: You can adjust properties like `line-height` to tweak text's typographic color and find an even gray that is neither too light nor too dark.

If you look at a page as a whole, you see that text is one element in a larger experience. Make sure your typography integrates as well as possible with that experience. To do this, you may need to adjust your text's overall color to keep things in balance with your page and site interface.

Finding a good balance could mean adjusting the actual hue of the text. For instance, text set as dark gray (e.g., #333) is often more comfortable to read on screen than full-black text. And other times, you may play with the `line-height` of paragraphs or the spacing of elements to create a harmonious lockup. There isn't always a method to determine these things, and many times designers nudge things a little or play with element values incrementally to see what works best. Whatever your method, strive for an even tone and relationship among text, images, and page so that the elements all come together to support the design's message.

WHITESPACE

Despite what some clients may tell you, empty space in a design isn't space that's waiting to be filled with content or (gasp!) banner ads. Whitespace is just as important as your company logo. Claude Debussy once said that music is the space between notes. Similarly, good typography is as much about the space between the letters as the letters themselves.

Whitespace frames the content and provides structure to the page. And when it comes to articles, whitespace is an indispensable factor not only in giving the eye room to read, but also in creating a welcoming environment. If your pages are too cluttered, you're inviting the reader to head elsewhere.

In **FIG 6.12**, whitespace frames the content in the center, which provides focus for the eye. It also imbues the text with space to breathe, which in turn gives the reader comfort to enjoy reading. These small touches go a long way, and like most of the niceties of design, they aren't usually apparent unless they're missing. Whitespace is our design's picture frame and a watchful guardian against the ever-advancing forces of clutter.

Margins

Margins can appear between and around elements on the page, as well as at the boundaries of your layout. They aid readability

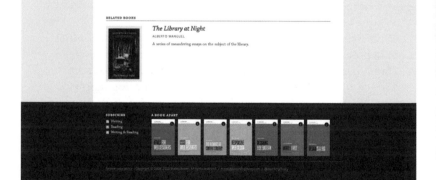

FIG 6.12: Mandy Brown's personal site, A Working Library, has ample whitespace to give readers room to enjoy reading (http://bkaprt.com/owt/65/).

FIG 6.13: It's common for books to have roomy side margins for thumb holds, but this also helps frame the content.

by differentiating elements from one another. I use the term *margin* generally here, as it doesn't matter if you're using CSS properties for margins, padding, or any other means of positioning. What matters is the amount of space between and around the elements.

If you're reading this book as a paperback, you'll notice a bit more space on the outside of the pages than the inside. That extra space is a direct nod to the print medium. You need space for your thumbs to hold the book without covering text (**FIG 6.13**). Obviously, we don't have that same constraint on a screen, but that space also supplies breathing room for the text, not just thumbs. Without a healthy margin around our text, our words will feel congested like a highway on-ramp at rush hour.

In general, I like to allot at least around 1.5-2 ems of margin around body text. Depending on the text's size and proximity to other page elements, you may need more of a margin or be able to get away with less.

TYPOGRAPHIC SCALES AND RHYTHM

Devising a system for sizing and spacing your typography has many advantages. It standardizes a method to your typographic madness in a reproducible way, enables consistency across a team of designers, and can make a lone designer's job easier by creating a framework.

When it comes to sizing, most designers fall into one of two camps: those who like to eyeball their type and those who prefer to arrange a sizing scale. I'm a chronic eyeballer, but I sometimes use scales to rough out sizing relationships.

Scales, often based on music signatures or ratios like the golden section (1:1.61803399), are used to create a palette of size options. For instance, let's look at the Fibonacci sequence, where each number is the sum of the previous two: 0, 1, 1, 2, 3, 5, 8, 13, 21, 34, 55, 89, 144, 233, 377, 610, 987, and so on. Since those numbers have built-in relationships with each other, you can pluck your sizing choices straight from that lineup. For instance, you could set your type at 13px and your headings at 34px. Moving higher on the scale, you could pick 987px for your layout width, with a main column of 610px and a sidebar of 377px.

Hop along that scale as you need—and think of the numbers as pant sizes. They all do the same thing (dress your legs); you just need to choose the one that suits your situation (your waist and height) the best (**FIG 6.14**).

Alternatively, you could start with a base type size and then apply a ratio to create a custom scale. Say your design's basic type and paragraphs read comfortably at 18 pixels when set in Chaparral. Using the same ratio as above (1:1.61803399), your resulting scale looks like: 6.876, 11.125, 18, 29.124, 47.123, and so on. As before, you can size other elements moving up and down the scale as you please.

In Tim Brown's *A List Apart* article "More Meaningful Typography," he argues that starting with a text size like this, and including another meaningful number from your design like a text column's width or a large headline's type size, creates a relevant and flexible modular scale for sizing (http://bkaprt. com/owt/66/). Tim even made a handy site called Modular Scale

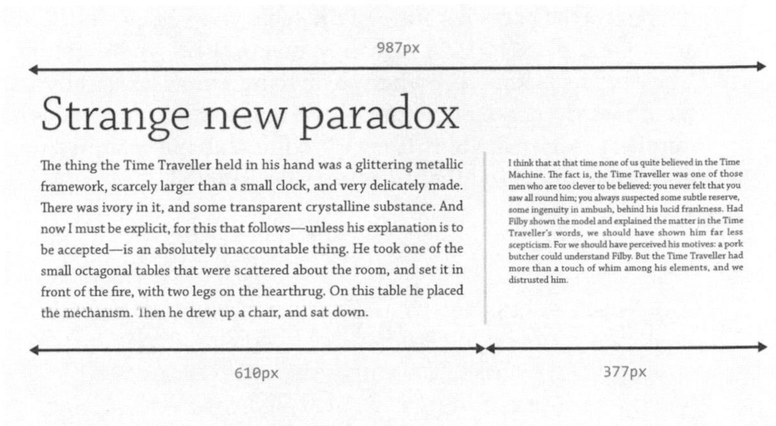

Strange new paradox

The thing the Time Traveller held in his hand was a glittering metallic framework, scarcely larger than a small clock, and very delicately made. There was ivory in it, and some transparent crystalline substance. And now I must be explicit, for this that follows—unless his explanation is to be accepted—is an absolutely unaccountable thing. He took one of the small octagonal tables that were scattered about the room, and set it in front of the fire, with two legs on the hearthrug. On this table he placed the mechanism. Then he drew up a chair, and sat down.

I think that at that time none of us quite believed in the Time Machine. The fact is, the Time Traveller was one of those men who are too clever to be believed: you never felt that you saw all round him; you always suspected some subtle reserve, some ingenuity in ambush, behind his lucid frankness. Had Filby shown the model and explained the matter in the Time Traveller's words, we should have shown him far less scepticism. For we should have perceived his motives: a pork butcher could understand Filby. But the Time Traveller had more than a touch of whim among his elements, and we distrusted him.

610px   377px

FIG 6.14: A simple layout based on a scale.

(http://bkaprt.com/owt/67/) that calculates the math for an array of scale ratios. A ratio has definite appeal: it helps rationalize and constrain the choices we make into a formula that we can apply throughout the design. Plus, it gives our design elements an underlying relationship. Our readers may never be aware of it, but a considered connection between everything exists, and that can sometimes make a design feel more cohesive.

But there is a small problem to be wary of when designing this way: it's very easy to become bound to the numbers instead of what looks appropriate.

As we learned earlier, finding typographic common ground between browsers can be a struggle, and typefaces of the same size don't always take up the same visual space. These are not fixed elements like bricks in a wall. Typefaces are unique and need to be considered uniquely in the context of their design. Typography is not always about numbers. While the crispness of numbers is appealing, what's important in typography is how something *looks and reads*. And designing by the numbers may not always get you there.

My starting point is often some scale, whether historically inspired or not, but I rarely adhere to it as I develop my design system. You should always evaluate your type in context, even if it resists the pristine nature of the scale you've devised. Scales are a great place to start, but they may not be where you finish. The key is knowing when to deviate. The visual results are what's important to refine, and those make more sense than the numbers. After all, your readers see the text and relationships, not the math behind them, as the end result.

CONCLUSION

As I proposed at the start of this book, everything in typographic design is connected. Like in *Powers of Ten*, the small pieces build the big pieces, and the big pieces are composed of the small pieces. The relationships they share can be approached from many different angles, but they are inextricably linked. Understanding these relationships gives you a deeper understanding of typography and the know-how to fiddle with the variables that affect it.

Just as there are no rules, the topics we've discussed are not an endpoint on typography for the screen. Breaking away from convention has been a massive part of typography's history, and often yields unexpected and interesting results. New methods, workarounds, and advancements are published online every day. But that's typography doing what it has always done: growing with the times and media as needs arise.

With practice, you'll find your own pathways and shortcuts without needing to use a formal process. You'll develop a gut instinct for what looks right or wrong typographically and you'll make critical judgements to arrive at your solutions faster.

Typography is a pursuit that combines the best of history, writing, math, artistry, and craft. No one thing rules over another. Sometimes the math won't add up, but the type may look right. When that happens, you need to rely on your instincts. Successful type will always be about the way something looks and the way something communicates. If you nail both of those things, you've done your job.

Trust your gut.

RESOURCES

Quick tips for improving your typography

- **When in doubt, make it bigger.** This is rarely true in design, but I've found it to be the case when designing for the screen. Err on the side of making your type too big rather than too small.
- **Create hierarchy.** Type embodies what you want to say with your design, and it creates and supports your website's structure. Use contrast, size, color, and placement to create a design system that prioritizes content to guide your readers.
- **Look for quality typefaces.** Just as buying fresh ingredients is a good way to start preparing a meal, finding quality typefaces is the first step toward good typography. Those typefaces may not be free, but they're often more sturdy and versatile than free options.
- **Limit your palette to one or two typefaces.** In my experience, the more typefaces I use in a design, the weaker the design becomes.
- **Pair a serif and a sans serif.** The inherent structural differences should present useful contrast, and you'll likely have enough options for styling various kinds of text elements.
- **Use proper quotation marks and apostrophes.** These are easy to miss and easy to forget, especially when your content moves from a text editor to a system that stumbles over proper quotation marks or swaps them for dumb quotes. Check and double-check that you have proper quotes, especially on headlines and big type.
- **Embrace space.** Space to read, space to breathe. The space that isn't occupied by text and imagery is often more important than the space that is. Whitespace gives readers time to rest their eyes, reflect, and reorient themselves.
- **Test and test again.** You can't expect your typography to look the same everywhere, but you can make sure it's legible and accessible. At a minimum, make sure you have a backup plan for when your fonts don't load.

Further reading and favorites

What follows are the books, websites, and type foundries I turn to time and again. If you're hungry for more information about typographic history, grids, or in-depth studies on typesetting, I urge you to take a look.
While many of these books approach typographic design from a print perspective, the techniques are transferable to the screen with a little extra consideration. The websites and type foundries often post about typeface releases and industry news.
Consider these as new starting points for your own typographic lineup.

Books

- *The Anatomy of Type: A Graphic Guide to 100 Typefaces,* Stephen Coles.
- *Book Typography: A Designer's Manual,* Michael Mitchell and Susan Wightman.
- *Combining Typefaces,* Tim Brown.
- *Detail in Typography,* Jost Hochuli.
- *The Elements of Typographic Style,* Robert Bringhurst.
- *Grid Systems in Graphic Design,* Josef Müller-Brockmann.
- *Inside Paragraphs: Typographic Fundamentals,* Cyrus Highsmith.
- *Making and Breaking the Grid: A Graphic Design Layout Workshop,* Timothy Samara.
- *Stop Stealing Sheep & Find Out How Type Works,* Erik Spiekermann and E.M. Ginger.
- *Thinking with Type: A Critical Guide for Designers, Writers, Editors, & Students,* Ellen Lupton.
- *Type and Typography,* Phil Baines and Andrew Haslam.
- *Type on Screen: A Critical Guide for Designers, Writers, Developers, & Students,* Ellen Lupton.
- *Understanding Comics: The Invisible Art,* Scott McCloud.

Websites

- A List Apart, typography tag, http://bkaprt.com/owt/68/
- Can I use..., http://bkaprt.com/owt/69/

- FontsInUse, http://bkaprt.com/owt/70/
- I Love Typography, http://bkaprt.com/owt/71/
- MyFonts, http://bkaprt.com/owt/72/
- Practical Typography, http://bkaprt.com/owt/73/
- Tobias Frere-Jones, http://bkaprt.com/owt/74/
- Type Sample, http://bkaprt.com/owt/75/
- Typecast, http://bkaprt.com/owt/76/
- Typedia, http://bkaprt.com/owt/77/
- Typekit blog, http://bkaprt.com/owt/78/
- Typekit Practice, http://bkaprt.com/owt/79/
- Typographica, http://bkaprt.com/owt/80/
- Webtype blog, http://bkaprt.com/owt/81/

Foundries and services

- Bold Monday, http://bkaprt.com/owt/82/
- Commercial Type, http://bkaprt.com/owt/83/
- Darden Studio, http://bkaprt.com/owt/84/
- Font Bureau, http://bkaprt.com/owt/85/
- FontShop, http://bkaprt.com/owt/86/
- Hoefler & Co., http://bkaprt.com/owt/87/
- House Industries, http://bkaprt.com/owt/88/
- HVD, http://bkaprt.com/owt/89/
- Just Another Foundry, http://bkaprt.com/owt/90/
- Klim Type Foundry, http://bkaprt.com/owt/91/
- The League of Movable Type, http://bkaprt.com/owt/92/
- Lost Type Co-op, http://bkaprt.com/owt/93/
- Mark Simonson Studio, http://bkaprt.com/owt/94/
- MVB, http://bkaprt.com/owt/95/
- Okay Type, http://bkaprt.com/owt/96/
- p.s.type, http://bkaprt.com/owt/97/
- Sudtipos, http://bkaprt.com/owt/98/
- Suitcase Type Foundry, http://bkaprt.com/owt/99/
- TypeTogether, http://bkaprt.com/owt/100/
- TypeTrust, http://bkaprt.com/owt/101/
- Typekit, http://bkaprt.com/owt/102/
- Typofonderie, http://bkaprt.com/owt/103/
- Underware, http://bkaprt.com/owt/104/
- Webtype, http://bkaprt.com/owt/105/

ACKNOWLEDGEMENTS

This book was tough on me. I foolishly imagined it would take me about six months to draft up, and here I am years later with considerably more gray hair. The fact that this book exists is in large part due to the help, ideas, support, and—most important—patience selflessly imparted by friends and colleagues. I've learned that writing a book takes a village.

My deepest thanks to Jeffrey Zeldman for taking me under his wing many years ago and always being there for me as an inspiration, mentor, and friend. Tina Lee and Mandy Brown, the best editors I can imagine, make me sound like a much better writer than I am and also constantly pushed for clarity in communication. The good parts of this book are likely good because of them. Katel LeDu seems superhumanly unflappable and was the guiding light during this whole process. Nick Sherman made sure I kept my foot out of my mouth and helped with numerous figures and references; he remains one of the sharpest typographic minds in our industry. Nicole Fenton and Caren Litherland made astute observations while editing and found the right spaces between the words. I'm also grateful to the entire A Book Apart family of colleagues and authors for making this library possible.

My closest friends are humble folks who would deny that they helped at all, but I get the last word, so there. Rob Weychert introduced me to graphic design and typography back in college, and he remains one of the most generous and thoughtful designers I've ever known. Liz Danzico is a dear friend and cohort who makes inquisitiveness an art; she taught me to try things I don't know how to do. Frank Chimero is wise and resourceful beyond his years, always quick with a helping hand, keen advice, or pizza party.

Thank you to Jeff Veen and the entire staff at Typekit for teaching me how to work quickly without being afraid to fall down. Professor Elaine Cunfer gave me my first A on a project and made me realize I wasn't a screwup.

Sympathy is extended to readers of embarrassing early drafts, and to friends who put up with me perpetually being a month away from done: Tim Brown, Leah Chamberlain,

Stephen Coles, Kevin Cornell, Kim Cornell, Chris Coyier, Greg Hoy, Grant Hutchinson, Erin Kissane, Jenn Lukas, Ethan Marcotte, Matt Sutter, Allen Tan, Trent Walton, David Yee, and my Studiomates—you are all saints and I will totally help you move or pick you up from the airport.

Thanks to Amtrak for always having an open seat on the Northeast Corridor for me to longingly look out the window from while I wrote, but not to New York's Penn Station, where imagination and happiness go to die.

I am honored that Ellen Lupton wrote this book's foreword. Her prolific work, writing, and teaching have influenced me more than I can put into words.

Thanks to my family: Mom and Dad, Pete, Marina, Giancarlo, and my grandparents for your unconditional support, even when I can't explain what I do all day—you mean everything to me.

Finally, I owe so much to my partner, Megan Born. You inspire me, make me laugh, and put up with my dumb jokes and freak-outs, all with an open heart and mind. I love you always.

REFERENCES

Shortened URLs are numbered sequentially; the related long URLs are listed below for reference.

Intro

1 http://youtube.com/watch?v=0fKBhvDjuy0

Chapter 1

2 https://twitter.com/typographica/status/268091875746009088

Chapter 2

3 http://alistapart.com/articles/responsive-web-design/
4 http://paulirish.com/2009/bulletproof-font-face-implementation-syntax/

Chapter 3

5 http://typographica.org/features/our-favorite-typefaces-of-2007/#comment-37743

6 http://fontawesome.io/

7 http://filamentgroup.com/lab/bulletproof_icon_fonts.html

8 http://css-tricks.com/icon-fonts-vs-svg/

9 http://kupferschrift.de/cms/2012/03/on-classifications/

10 http://typedia.com/blog/post/torch-drawing-letters/

11 http://bobulate.com/

12 http://opentype.info/blog/2012/04/10/x-height-and-legibility/

13 http://caniuse.com/#feat=font-feature

14 http://typography.com/cloud/

15 http://smartquotesforsmartpeople.com/

16 http://quotesandaccents.com/

17 http://w3.org/TR/css3-fonts/

18 http://typography.com/fonts/gotham/features/gotham-language-support/

19 http://fontbureau.com/ReadingEdge/

20 http://en.wikipedia.org/wiki/Garamond#Jean_Jannon_misattribution

21 http://observatory.designobserver.com/entry.html?entry=2577

22 https://developers.google.com/fonts/docs/webfont_loader

23 http://blog.typekit.com/2011/05/25/loading-typekit-fonts-asynchronously/

24 http://blog.typekit.com/2010/10/15/type-rendering-operating-systems/

25 http://joelonsoftware.com/items/2007/06/12.html

26 http://blog.typekit.com/2011/01/26/css-properties-that-affect-type-rendering/

27 http://blog.typekit.com/2010/10/05/type-rendering-on-the-web/

28 https://typotheque.com/articles/hinting/

Chapter 4

29 http://fiftythree.com/pencil

30 http://gmunch.home.pipeline.com/typo-L/misc/ward.htm

31 http://storiesandnovels.com/buster.php

32 http://madebymighty.com/

33 http://articles.latimes.com/2008/mar/30/image/ig-font30

34 http://blog.fontdeck.com/post/23601339698/body-text-tester

35 http://typecast.com/

36 http://webfonter.fontshop.com/

37 http://webtype.com/tools/swapper/

38 http://aiga.org/the-mostly-true-story-of-helvetica-and-the-new-york-city-subway/

39 http://nytimes.com/2004/07/08/nyregion/08blocks.html

40 http://fontsinuse.com/

41 https://typesupply.com/news/2013/9/the-development-of-balto

42 http://fontshop.com/blog/newsletters/june10a/indexEMAIL.html

43 http://fount.artequalswork.com/

44 http://myfonts.com/WhatTheFont/

45 http://identifont.com/

46 http://ilovetypography.com/

47 http://jasonsantamaria.com/

Chapter 5

48 http://wm4.wilsonminer.com/posts/2008/oct/20/relative-readability/

49 http://j.eremy.net/confused-about-rem-and-em/

50 http://css-tricks.com/almanac/properties/l/line-height/

51 http://trentwalton.com/2013/02/07/where-to-start/

52 http://siteleaf.com/

53 http://fittextjs.com/

54 http://font-to-width.com/
55 http://letteringjs.com/
56 http://css-tricks.com/viewport-sized-typography/
57 http://bobulate.com/post/22192501341/a-shape-of-design
58 http://theverge.com/2013/6/6/4394808/brian-vaughan-marcos-martin-interview
59 http://kottke.org/13/06/ethan-hawke-answers-some-questions
60 http://typecast.com/

Chapter 6

61 http://trentwalton.com/2012/06/19/fluid-type/
62 http://subtraction.com/
63 http://thegridsystem.org/
64 http://jasonsantamaria.com/articles/the-space-between-the-notes/
65 http://aworkinglibrary.com/writing/on-the-library/index.html
66 http://alistapart.com/article/more-meaningful-typography/
67 http://modularscale.com/

Resources

68 http://alistapart.com/topic/typography-web-fonts/
69 http://caniuse.com/
70 http://fontsinuse.com/
71 http://ilovetypography.com/
72 http://myfonts.com/
73 http://practicaltypography.com/
74 http://frerejones.com/
75 http://typesample.com/
76 http://typecast.com/
77 http://typedia.com/
78 http://blog.typekit.com/
79 http://practice.typekit.com/
80 http://typographica.org/
81 http://blog.webtype.com/
82 http://boldmonday.com/
83 https://commercialtype.com/
84 http://dardenstudio.com/
85 http://fontbureau.com/

86 http://fontshop.com/
87 http://typography.com/
88 http://houseind.com/
89 http://hvdfonts.com/
90 http://justanotherfoundry.com/
91 https://klim.co.nz/
92 http://theleagueofmoveabletype.com/
93 http://losttype.com/
94 http://marksimonson.com/
95 http://mvbfonts.com/
96 http://okaytype.com/
97 http://cargocollective.com/pstype/
98 http://sudtipos.com/
99 http://suitcasetype.com/
100 http://type-together.com/
101 http://typetrust.com/
102 http://typekit.com/
103 http://typofonderie.com/
104 http://underware.nl/
105 http://webtype.com/

INDEX

ABOUT A BOOK APART

We cover the emerging and essential topics in web design and development with style, clarity, and above all, brevity—because working designer-developers can't afford to waste time.

COLOPHON

The text is set in FF Yoga and its companion, FF Yoga Sans, both by Xavier Dupré. Headlines and cover are set in Titling Gothic by David Berlow.

MIX
Paper from responsible sources
FSC® C103203

This book was printed in the United States using FSC certified Finch papers.